Universal Humanity: Embracing the World

Mostafa Maleki Tehrani

Firouz Media 2024

Firouz Media Limited have contributed to the publication of this book, while the author retains full responsibility for copyright, content accuracy, and any legal matters. This book is a testament to the author's commitment and enthusiasm, and our involvement represents a collaborative hybrid effort in publishing. As you immerse yourself in its contents, we sincerely hope you find inspiration, insight, and delight.

ISBN 978-1-915557-18-6
www.firouzmedia.com
IG: @firouzmedia

Cover picture: Arif_Vector
Stock images: Pexels_Adobe_Pixabay

Universal Humanity: Embracing the World
Creator: Mostafa Maleki Tehrani

Preface

When the three words "human", "world", and "cosmos" come together, they provide a definition that transcends their individual meanings, implying a collective whole greater than the sum of its parts. This suggests the need for deeper examination and contemplation within this context. In today's era, where interactions between machines and humans replace many human relationships, it's important to understand the characteristics of a cosmopolitan human and strive to strengthen them. Otherwise, we risk losing the constructive power of interaction, first with oneself and then with others, leading to confusion and depression.

If in ancient times geographical boundaries and cultural interpretations were the factors influencing the expansion and interpretation of communication, today the disappearance of language, geographical borders, and cultural barriers, moving towards unity amidst diversity, has accelerated the process of globalizing humans. In this transitional phase, it is imperative to educate individuals about the characteristics of the modern human.

In many books and articles, the issue has been discussed in detail, but the clarification of its characteristics in simple and understandable language for the general public has been undertaken by the McGraw Hill Education. Here, I have tried to provide a comprehensive and concise definition for each feature, in addition to mentioning the titles of those characteristics for each command. Since the field of discussion is human resources and within this space, different individuals can have different definitions of an issue, it is undoubtedly possible that some of the explanations may not be acceptable to experts. It is the place of experts to guide me initially and then to help improve the content of this book and my other writings. The latest topic is about worldview. It is assumed that human and ethical worldview is the basis of our definitions. Otherwise, everything mentioned may be different from what it should be. I would like to thank the kindness of the professors and friends who accompanied me on this journey.

—Mostafa Maleki Tehrani

Vlado Paunovic

Abstraction in Speech & Thought

Refers to the ability to conceptualize ideas, objects, or phenomena beyond their immediate physical or sensory manifestations. It involves the capacity to think in general terms, extract essential qualities, and formulate overarching concepts.
This cognitive process allows humans to communicate complex ideas and understandings effectively.

Aesthetics

Refers to the branch of philosophy that explores concepts of beauty, art, and taste. It encompasses the study of sensory experiences, emotional responses, and the principles underlying artistic creation and appreciation. Aesthetics examines the nature of aesthetic judgments, cultural influences on perceptions of beauty, and the role of art in human life. It also explores the relationship between form and content, as well as the criteria for evaluating artistic expression.

Actions Under Self-control Distinguished from Those Not Under Control

Pertains to the ability of individuals to regulate their behavior consciously. Actions under self-control are those in which individuals make deliberate decisions based on their values, goals, and principles, whereas actions not under control are impulsive or involuntary responses driven by external influences or internal urges. This distinction highlights the importance of self-awareness and intentional decision-making in human behavior.

Affection Expressed and Felt

Encompasses both the outward demonstration and internal experience of fondness, warmth, and caring towards others. It involves the communication of love, compassion, and empathy through gestures, words, and actions. Affection expressed can include verbal affirmations, physical gestures like hugs or kisses, and acts of kindness. Affection felt refers to the emotional experience of attachment and connection, which may manifest as feelings of closeness, security, and happiness in relationships. It's a fundamental aspect of human bonding and social interaction.

Attachment

Refers to the emotional bond or connection formed between individuals, typically between caregivers and infants but also applicable to adult relationships. It involves feelings of security, comfort, and trust that develop through consistent care, responsiveness, and interaction. Attachment theory, developed by John Bowlby and Mary Ainsworth, suggests that early experiences with caregivers shape individuals' attachment styles, which influence their relationships and social interactions throughout life. Secure attachment is characterized by a strong sense of trust and intimacy, while insecure attachment may lead to difficulties in forming close relationships or managing emotions effectively.

Age Grades, Age Statuses, and Age Terms

Refer to various social constructs and classifications based on chronological age within a given society or culture.

- *Age Grades*: Social groupings based on age that dictate roles and responsibilities in a community.
- *Age Statuses*: Social positions assigned according to age, determining rights and duties within society.
- *Age Terms*: Linguistic expressions denoting different stages of life based on age, reflecting societal attitudes and values.

These concepts are essential for understanding how societies organize and structure social interactions, roles, and expectations based on age-related factors. They play a significant role in shaping individuals' identities and experiences at different stages of life.

Scott Webb

Ambivalence

Refers to the coexistence of conflicting emotions, attitudes, or opinions towards a particular person, object, or situation. It involves feeling both positive and negative sentiments simultaneously, making it challenging to make a clear decision or take definitive action. Ambivalence is a common human experience and can arise in various contexts, such as relationships, career choices, or moral dilemmas. It often reflects the complexity and nuances of human emotions and cognition.

"Anthropomorphization" is the attribution of human characteristics, behaviors, or emotions to non-human entities, such as animals, objects, or natural phenomena. It involves interpreting and describing non-human entities in terms of human traits or experiences, often to facilitate understanding or emotional connection. Anthropomorphization is a common phenomenon in literature, art, and popular culture, where animals or objects are portrayed with human-like qualities to evoke empathy, humor, or relatability.

"Anticipation" refers to the act of looking forward to or expecting something in the future. It involves mentally preparing for an upcoming event, situation, or outcome, often accompanied by a sense of excitement, eagerness, or apprehension. Anticipation plays a crucial role in human decision-making, planning, and motivation, as it influences how individuals set goals, allocate resources, and manage their expectations. It can enhance the enjoyment of positive experiences and help individuals cope with uncertainty or adversity by mentally preparing for potential challenges.

"Antonyms" are words that have opposite meanings or convey contrasting ideas. They provide linguistic contrast and are often used to express nuances in language or to emphasize differences between concepts. Understanding antonyms is essential for effective communication, as they allow for precise expression and help convey specific shades of meaning. Examples of antonyms include hot and cold, happy and sad, and light and dark.

Beliefs

Belief in Supernatural/Religion: The acceptance of the existence of supernatural forces or beings, often associated with religious faith and practices. This belief system encompasses faith in deities, spirits, divine intervention, and religious rituals, shaping individuals' worldview, values, and behaviors.

False Beliefs: Erroneous or unfounded convictions held by individuals despite evidence or rational arguments to the contrary. False beliefs can stem from misinformation, cognitive biases, or cultural influences, leading to misunderstandings, superstitions, or pseudoscientific beliefs.

Beliefs about Death: Views, attitudes, and interpretations regarding the nature, significance, and afterlife of death. These beliefs vary widely across cultures and religions, influencing funeral customs, mourning rituals, and perceptions of mortality and the afterlife.

Beliefs about Disease: Perspectives, explanations, and attitudes regarding the causes, nature, and treatment of illness and disease. These beliefs encompass cultural, religious, and folk explanations of health and illness, affecting healthcare-seeking behaviors, treatment adherence, and stigma associated with certain conditions.

Beliefs about Fortune and Misfortune: Convictions about luck, fate, and the attribution of positive or negative events in life. These beliefs encompass notions of destiny, karma, providence, and the role of personal agency in shaping one's fortunes. They influence decision-making, coping strategies, and perceptions of success and adversity.

"Baby talk," also known as infant-directed speech or motherese, is a form of communication characterized by simplified vocabulary, exaggerated intonation, and repetitive patterns, typically used when speaking to infants and young children. This style of speech is instinctively adopted by caregivers across cultures and serves several purposes, including capturing infants' attention, facilitating language development, and fostering emotional bonding.
Baby talk features high-pitched tones, elongated vowels, and rhythmic patterns, which are believed to enhance infants' comprehension and engagement. While it may sound nonsensical to adults, baby talk plays a vital role in early language acquisition and social interaction.

Amanda Elizabeth

"Binary cognitive distinctions"

Refer to the categorization of concepts or ideas into two distinct and opposing categories. This cognitive framework simplifies complex phenomena by dividing them into mutually exclusive and exhaustive categories, allowing for clearer understanding and communication. Examples of binary cognitive distinctions include good vs. bad, true vs. false, right vs. wrong, and black vs. white. While binary thinking can provide clarity and structure, it may oversimplify reality and overlook nuances or shades of grey.

"Biological mother and social mother" are terms used to distinguish between two different roles in a child's life.

Biological Mother: The biological mother is the woman who gave birth to the child. She is genetically related to the child and may or may not have an active role in the child's upbringing or care. The biological mother's role in the child's life can vary depending on factors such as custody arrangements, family dynamics, and personal circumstances.

Social Mother: The social mother is the woman who assumes the primary caregiving role and responsibility for the child's upbringing and well-being, regardless of biological relation. This individual may be a stepmother, adoptive mother, foster mother, or other caregiver who fulfills the maternal role in the child's life. The social mother provides emotional support, nurturance, guidance, and protection to the child, often forming a strong bond and attachment similar to that of a biological mother.

"Normally the same person" refers to the common scenario where the roles of biological mother and social mother are fulfilled by one individual. In many cases, the woman who gives birth to a child also assumes the primary caregiving role and responsibility for the child's upbringing, forming both the biological and social mother. This alignment of roles occurs naturally in many families and is typical in traditional family structures. However, in situations such as adoption, surrogacy, or blended families, the roles of biological and social mother may be fulfilled by different individuals.

"Body adornment" refers to the practice of decorating or modifying the human body for aesthetic, cultural, social, or religious purposes. This can include wearing jewelry, clothing, makeup, tattoos, piercings, or other accessories to enhance one's appearance or express personal identity. Body adornment has been practiced by various cultures throughout history, serving as a form of self-expression, social signaling, or group affiliation. It reflects individual tastes, cultural traditions, and societal norms, playing a significant role in shaping personal and collective identities.

"The creation of a human, and love are the closest proximity to God"
A sentiment often found in religious or spiritual beliefs. It suggests that the act of human creation, whether understood in religious, philosophical, or metaphorical terms, represents a profound connection to divinity or the divine. This idea underscores the significance and sanctity attributed to human life and existence, emphasizing the inherent value and potential inherent in each individual. It reflects the belief in the divine spark or essence within each human being, highlighting the special role that humans play in the grand scheme of existence.

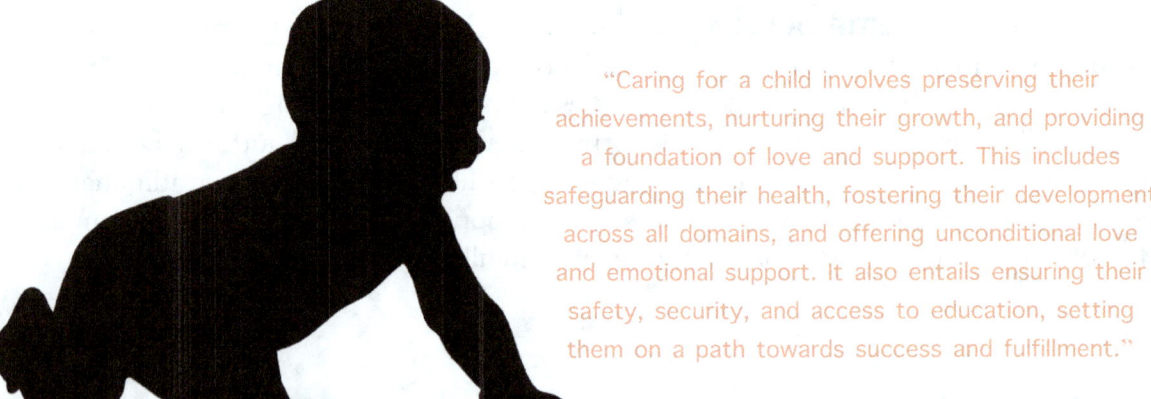

"Caring for a child involves preserving their achievements, nurturing their growth, and providing a foundation of love and support. This includes safeguarding their health, fostering their development across all domains, and offering unconditional love and emotional support. It also entails ensuring their safety, security, and access to education, setting them on a path towards success and fulfillment."

"Childbirth customs" and "Reproduction culture"
are related but distinct concepts:

Childbirth Customs: These refer specifically to the cultural practices, rituals, and traditions surrounding the process of giving birth and the postpartum period. They focus on the practices and beliefs associated with pregnancy, labor and delivery, and the care of the mother and newborn immediately after birth. Childbirth customs often involve rituals, ceremonies, and practical measures aimed at supporting the mother, welcoming the newborn, and integrating the new addition into the family and community.

Reproduction Culture: This encompasses a broader set of beliefs, values, norms, and practices related to human reproduction and family planning within a given society or culture. While childbirth customs are part of reproduction culture, reproduction culture also includes attitudes and behaviors regarding contraception, fertility, abortion, adoption, family size, gender roles in reproduction, and the social and cultural significance of reproduction. It extends beyond the immediate childbirth experience to encompass the broader social and cultural context in which reproductive decisions are made and acted upon.

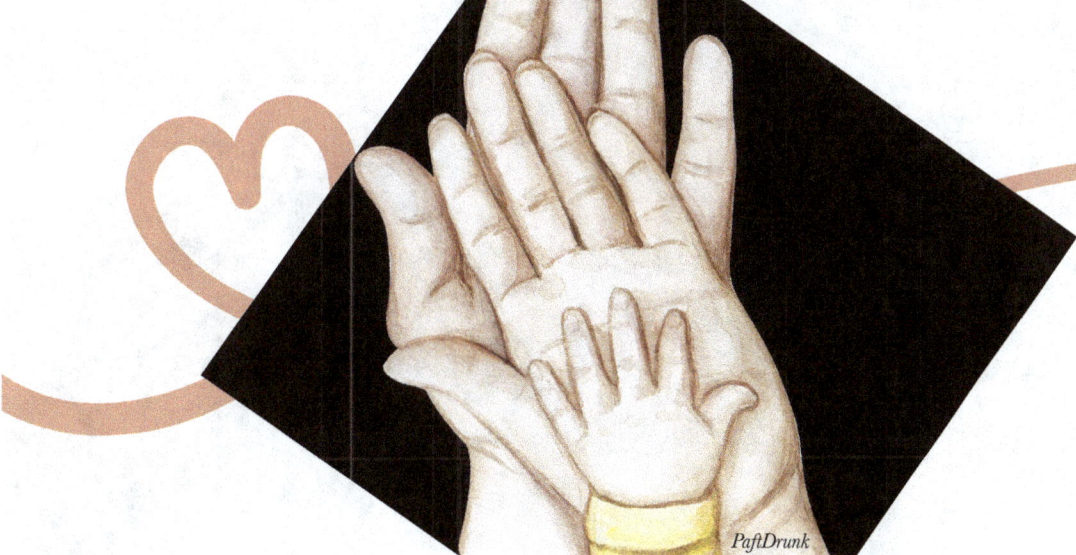

Embracing the World | 13

"Childhood fears", such as a fear of loud noises or strangers, are common experiences among young children as they navigate the world and develop their understanding of it.

Childhood Fear of Loud Noises: Many children exhibit a fear of loud noises, which can stem from a natural sensitivity to sudden or unexpected sounds. This fear may manifest as crying, hiding, or seeking comfort from caregivers when exposed to loud noises such as thunderstorms, fireworks, or household appliances. It often diminishes as children grow wolder and develop coping mechanisms to manage their reactions to loud sounds.

Childhood Fear of Strangers: A fear of strangers is another common childhood fear, characterized by anxiety or apprehension when encountering unfamiliar people. This fear may arise from a lack of trust in unknown individuals or from concerns about potential danger or harm. Children may exhibit avoidance behaviors, clinginess to caregivers, or expressions of distress when approached by strangers. Strategies such as teaching children about personal safety, practicing social skills, and gradually exposing them to new people in safe environments can help alleviate this fear over time.

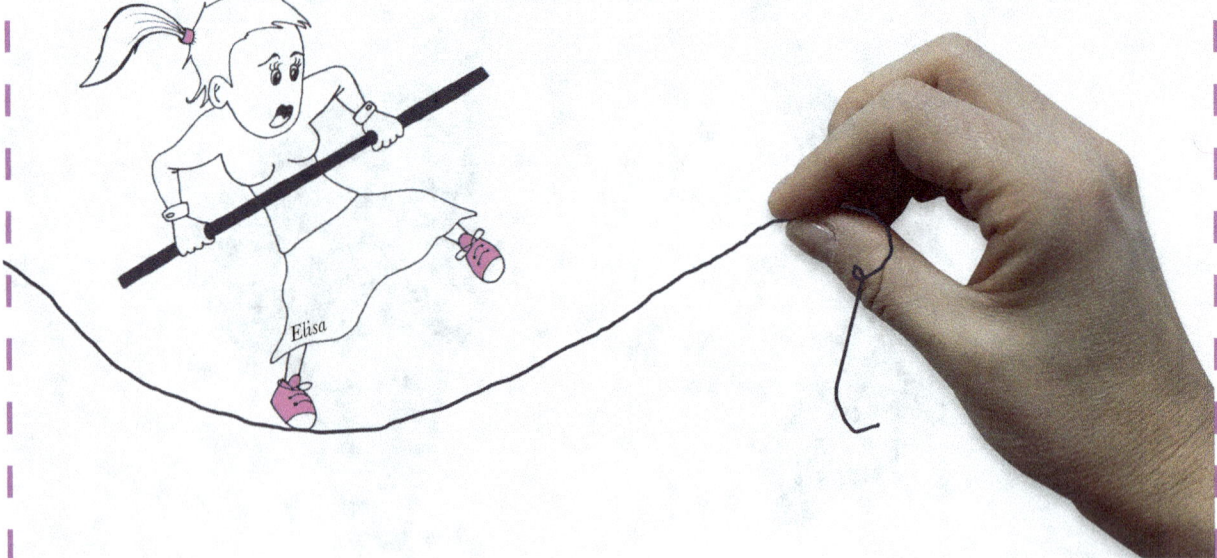

"Classification" refers to the process of categorizing or organizing things into groups based on similarities or shared characteristics. In the context of your book, it could involve classifying different aspects of humanity, such as cultural backgrounds, belief systems, or social structures, in order to better understand and embrace the diversity within the global human community.

- classification of age
- classification of behavioral propensities
- classification of body parts
- classification of colors
- classification of fauna
- classification of flora
- classification of inner states
- classification of kin
- classification of sex
- classification of space
- classification of tools
- classification of weather conditions

"Choice making," specifically in the context of "choosing alternatives," refers to the cognitive process of evaluating available options and selecting one among them. This process involves weighing the pros and cons of each alternative, considering personal preferences, values, and goals, and making a decision that aligns with one's objectives or needs. Choice making is a fundamental aspect of daily life and can range from simple decisions, such as what to eat for breakfast, to complex decisions, such as choosing a career path or making financial investments. Effective choice making requires critical thinking, problem-solving skills, and self-awareness to navigate the multitude of options and make informed decisions that lead to desired outcomes.

"Collective identities" are the shared characteristics, values, beliefs, and experiences that bind individuals together within a group or community. These identities can be based on various factors such as nationality, ethnicity, religion, or shared interests. Understanding and respecting collective identities is crucial for fostering unity and cooperation among diverse groups of people on a global scale.

"Conflict" refers to a disagreement or clash between individuals, groups, or nations arising from differences in interests, values, or beliefs. In the context of your book, exploring conflicts and their resolutions is essential for promoting understanding and harmony among people from diverse backgrounds. Understanding the root causes of conflicts and learning effective conflict resolution strategies can contribute to building a more peaceful and inclusive world.

"Conjectural reasoning" involves making educated guesses or hypotheses based on incomplete information or evidence. It's a cognitive process where individuals use reasoning and inference to draw conclusions about uncertain situations. In your book, discussing conjectural reasoning can highlight the importance of critical thinking and creativity in navigating complex issues and uncertainties in the modern world. It can also emphasize the need for humility and openness to new perspectives when dealing with ambiguous or unknown situations.

"Containers" can refer to physical objects used for holding or transporting items, but in a broader sense, it can also represent conceptual frameworks or boundaries that shape our understanding of the world. In your book, exploring the idea of "containers" could involve examining how societal norms, cultural boundaries, and mental constructs influence our perceptions and interactions with others. Understanding these containers and their implications can help individuals expand their worldview and embrace greater inclusivity and empathy towards diverse perspectives.

"Continua" (ordering as cognitive pattern), refers to the cognitive process of arranging concepts, ideas, or experiences along a continuous spectrum or scale.
This pattern of thinking involves recognizing and understanding the gradations or degrees of variation between different elements rather than viewing them as discrete categories.
In your book, exploring continua as a cognitive pattern can highlight the interconnectedness and fluidity of human experiences and identities, encouraging readers to embrace complexity and nuance in their understanding of the world.

"Contrasting Marked and Unmarked Memes" (meaningful elements in language), involves examining the linguistic concept of markedness, which refers to the presence or absence of certain features that contribute to the meaning or interpretation of words, phrases, or symbols. In language, marked elements are those that deviate from the norm or default form (unmarked), often carrying additional connotations or emphasis. Exploring this concept in your book can help readers understand how language shapes perception and communication, and how marked and unmarked elements contribute to the richness and complexity of human expression.

"Copulation Normally Conducted in Privacy" refers to the societal norm or expectation that sexual intercourse typically occurs in private settings, away from public view. This cultural convention varies across different societies and is often influenced by factors such as social norms, religious beliefs, and legal regulations. Respecting the privacy of individuals' intimate activities is considered a fundamental aspect of human dignity and personal autonomy. In your book, discussing this concept can contribute to the exploration of cultural norms surrounding sexuality and privacy, as well as the importance of consent and respect in intimate relationships.

"Cooking" is the process of preparing food through various techniques such as heating, mixing, and seasoning to make it suitable for consumption. It is both a practical skill and a form of creative expression, deeply rooted in cultural traditions and individual preferences. In addition to providing nourishment, cooking can also serve as a means of social bonding, cultural exchange, and personal fulfillment. Exploring the art and science of cooking in your book can highlight its role in promoting cultural diversity, health, and well-being, as well as its potential to foster connection and understanding among people from different backgrounds.

Klaus Nielsen

wixin lubhon

Embracing the World | 19

"Cooperation" is the act of working together towards a common goal or objective. It involves individuals or groups willingly collaborating, sharing resources, and coordinating their efforts to achieve mutual benefits. Cooperation is essential for fostering harmony, progress, and mutual understanding among people, communities, and nations. In your book, exploring cooperation can highlight its significance in building inclusive societies, resolving conflicts, and addressing global challenges effectively through collective action and solidarity.

"Cooperative labor" involves individuals or groups working together in a collaborative manner to accomplish a task or achieve a common goal. Unlike individual labor, cooperative labor emphasizes collective effort, shared responsibility, and mutual support. This concept can be applied across various contexts, including agriculture, construction, community projects, and business ventures. In your book, discussing cooperative labor can underscore its importance in promoting teamwork, productivity, and social cohesion, as well as its potential to empower individuals and communities through collective action and mutual aid.

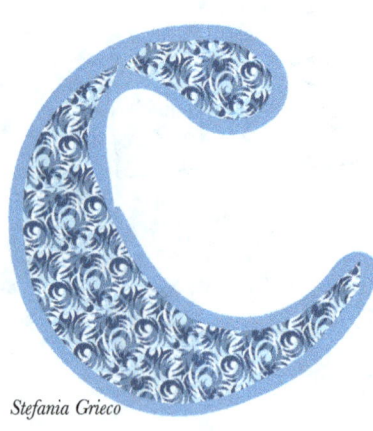

Stefania Grieco

"Corporate (perpetual) statuses" refers to the ongoing legal existence of corporations, which are separate legal entities from their owners or shareholders. The term "perpetual" indicates that corporations have a continuous existence, regardless of changes in ownership or leadership. This concept is a fundamental aspect of corporate law and allows corporations to enter into contracts, own property, and engage in business activities independently of their shareholders. Discussing corporate statuses in your book can provide insights into the legal framework and governance structures that govern corporate entities, as well as their rights, responsibilities, and obligations within society.

"Coyness Display" refers to a behavior characterized by a modest or shy reluctance to engage in certain actions or conversations, often in a playful or flirtatious manner. This behavior can involve subtle gestures, expressions, or verbal cues that convey a sense of reluctance or hesitation, while also hinting at interest or attraction.

In social interactions, coyness display can serve various purposes, such as signaling romantic interest, maintaining social decorum, or exerting control over the pace of a relationship. Exploring the dynamics of coyness display in your book can shed light on the complexities of human communication, gender roles, and interpersonal relationships.

"Crying" is a natural emotional response characterized by the shedding of tears, often accompanied by vocal sounds and facial expressions. It serves as a means of expressing a range of emotions, including sadness, grief, frustration, joy, or relief. Crying can have both physiological and psychological benefits, such as releasing stress hormones, eliciting empathy and support from others, and providing emotional catharsis. In your book, exploring the phenomenon of crying can shed light on the complexity of human emotions, the social and cultural significance of tears, and the importance of emotional expression in maintaining mental health and interpersonal connections.

Pixabay

"Critical learning periods" refer to specific developmental stages or phases in an individual's life when they are particularly receptive to acquiring certain skills, knowledge, or behaviors. These periods are characterized by heightened neuroplasticity and sensitivity to environmental stimuli, allowing for rapid and profound learning experiences. Critical learning periods are often associated with early childhood, adolescence, and other transitional phases in human development. In your book, discussing critical learning periods can highlight the importance of early education, lifelong learning, and the role of environment in shaping cognitive, social, and emotional development.

"culture/nature distinction" Refers to the conceptual separation between human-made or cultural phenomena and natural phenomena. It is a fundamental dichotomy in many philosophical, sociological, and environmental discourses, exploring the perceived boundaries and interactions between human activities and the natural world.

"Cultural variability" refers to the diversity and differences in beliefs, values, customs, behaviors, and practices across different cultures. It highlights the dynamic nature of human societies and the rich tapestry of cultural expressions that shape individuals' identities and experiences. Cultural variability can manifest in various aspects of life, including language, religion, family structure, social norms, and traditions. Understanding cultural variability is essential for promoting cross-cultural awareness, tolerance, and appreciation, as well as for navigating cultural differences and fostering intercultural communication and collaboration. In your book, exploring cultural variability can help readers recognize the complexity and richness of human diversity, challenging ethnocentric perspectives and promoting cultural sensitivity and respect.

"Culture"

encompasses the shared beliefs, values, customs, traditions, behaviors, and symbols that are characteristic of a particular group of people or society. It is a dynamic and multifaceted concept that shapes individuals' identities, worldview, and interactions within their social environment. Culture influences various aspects of life, including language, religion, art, music, cuisine, social norms, and institutions. It provides a framework for understanding the world, guiding social interactions, and transmitting knowledge from one generation to the next.

Pixabay

"Customary greetings" refer to the traditional or culturally appropriate ways of exchanging pleasantries and salutations when meeting or interacting with others. These greetings often vary widely across different cultures and can include verbal expressions, physical gestures, or a combination of both. Common examples of customary greetings include saying "hello," "good morning," or "how are you?" in spoken language, as well as gestures such as handshakes, hugs, bows, or kisses depending on the cultural context.

"Daily routines" refer to the regular and habitual activities that individuals engage in on a day-to-day basis. These routines often encompass a variety of tasks and behaviors, such as waking up, getting dressed, eating meals, going to work or school, exercising, socializing, and sleeping. Daily routines provide structure and organization to people's lives, helping them manage their time, accomplish tasks efficiently, and maintain a sense of stability and well-being.

"Dance" is a form of artistic expression and physical movement that encompasses a wide range of styles, techniques, and cultural traditions. It is a universal human activity that has been practiced throughout history as a means of communication, celebration, storytelling, ritual, and self-expression. Dance can take many forms, including ballet, modern dance, hip-hop, folk dance, traditional cultural dances, and social dances.

In addition to its artistic and cultural significance, dance also has numerous physical, mental, and emotional benefits. It promotes physical fitness, coordination, and flexibility, enhances cognitive function and memory, reduces stress and anxiety, and fosters social connections and community cohesion.

"Death rituals" are ceremonial practices and customs performed by individuals and communities to honor and commemorate the deceased. These rituals vary widely across different cultures, religions, and belief systems, but they often serve several common purposes: to acknowledge the death of a loved one, to provide comfort and support to the grieving, to facilitate the transition of the deceased to the afterlife or the next stage of existence, and to reaffirm cultural and spiritual beliefs about life and death.

Death rituals may include various activities such as funeral ceremonies, memorial services, cremation or burial rites, mourning rituals, and commemorative gatherings. They may also involve symbolic gestures, prayers, chants, music, dance, offerings, and rituals performed by religious or spiritual leaders.

"Collective decision-making" refers to the process by which a group of individuals come together to make choices or reach agreements on a particular course of action. This approach to decision-making involves pooling the knowledge, perspectives, and preferences of multiple stakeholders to arrive at a consensus or majority decision.

Collective decision-making can take various forms, ranging from informal discussions and consensus-building exercises to more structured processes such as voting, deliberative democracy, or participatory decision-making models. The effectiveness of collective decision-making depends on factors such as the size and composition of the group, the quality of communication and collaboration among members, the presence of facilitators or mediators, and the degree of inclusivity and transparency in the process.

"Differential valuations" refer to variations in the perceived worth or value of goods, services, or outcomes among different individuals or groups. These differences in valuation can arise from diverse factors such as personal preferences, cultural norms, economic considerations, and individual experiences.

In the context of decision-making, understanding differential valuations is crucial for assessing trade-offs, negotiating agreements, and resolving conflicts. Recognizing that individuals may assign different levels of importance or significance to various options can help facilitate compromise and consensus-building in collective decision-making processes.

"Giving directions" involves providing instructions or guidance to help someone navigate from one location to another. Effective directions typically include clear and concise information about landmarks, street names, turns, distances, and other relevant details to ensure the recipient can reach their destination successfully.

When giving directions, it's important to consider the perspective of the person receiving them, as they may have different levels of familiarity with the area or may prefer certain modes of navigation (e.g., verbal instructions, written directions, maps, or GPS). Tailoring directions to accommodate the recipient's needs and preferences can enhance their understanding and confidence in following them.

Pixabay

"Discrepancies between speech, thought, and action"

Refer to inconsistencies or mismatches that may occur between what individuals say, what they think, and how they behave in practice. These discrepancies can arise for various reasons, such as conflicting beliefs, social pressures, unconscious biases, or situational factors.

In some cases, individuals may express certain beliefs or intentions verbally but fail to follow through with corresponding actions. This discrepancy between speech and action can result from factors such as procrastination, lack of motivation, or external obstacles. Alternatively, individuals may behave in ways that contradict their stated beliefs or values, leading to a mismatch between their actions and their professed intentions.

Embracing the World | 27

"Dispersed groups" refer to collections of individuals who are geographically separated but connected through shared interests, goals, or affiliations. These groups may exist in various forms, including virtual teams, online communities, decentralized organizations, or global networks.

In dispersed groups, members typically communicate and collaborate using digital technologies such as email, video conferencing, instant messaging, and collaboration platforms. Despite physical distance, dispersed groups can leverage these tools to work together, share information, and coordinate activities effectively.

"Distinguishing right and wrong" involves the cognitive and ethical process of discerning between morally acceptable and unacceptable actions or behaviors. This ability to make moral judgments is influenced by a variety of factors, including cultural norms, religious beliefs, personal values, empathy, and reasoning abilities.

Individuals often rely on moral principles, ethical guidelines, and societal norms to help them determine what is right or wrong in a given situation. However, moral decision-making can be complex and subjective, as different people may prioritize different values or weigh conflicting considerations differently.

"Diurnality" refers to the behavioral pattern of being active primarily during the daytime and resting or sleeping during the nighttime. Organisms that exhibit diurnality are known as diurnal, and they have adapted their physiological and behavioral characteristics to optimize their activities and functions in accordance with the day-night cycle.

Diurnality is commonly observed in many species of animals, including humans, birds, and some mammals. It is often associated with factors such as the availability of light, temperature fluctuations, predator-prey interactions, and resource availability. Diurnal animals typically have specialized sensory adaptations, such as keen daytime vision or heightened activity levels during daylight hours, to maximize their foraging, hunting, or social interactions during the day.

"Divination" is the practice of seeking knowledge or insight about the future or unknown events through supernatural or mystical means. It has been a common practice across cultures and throughout history, often involving rituals, symbols, or techniques believed to facilitate communication with divine or spiritual forces.

Various methods of divination exist, including astrology, tarot card reading, palmistry, scrying (e.g., using a crystal ball or mirror), and consulting oracles (e.g., the I Ching or the Delphic Oracle). Each method has its own traditions, symbols, and interpretations, but they share the underlying belief that it is possible to gain insights or guidance beyond ordinary human perception.

The **"division of labor"** refers to how tasks and responsibilities are specialized within a group or society. People or groups focus on specific activities based on skills or resources. This specialization boosts productivity and efficiency but can lead to inequalities. It's key to understanding how economies and societies organize. Discussing it in your book can shed light on how societies function and the challenges they face in ensuring fairness and opportunity for all.

"Dominance/submission" is a social dynamic where individuals or groups assert control or authority (dominance) over others, who then yield or defer to this authority (submission). This dynamic can manifest in various contexts, including interpersonal relationships, social hierarchies, and organizational structures.

In interpersonal relationships, dominance/submission dynamics may involve power imbalances, where one person exerts influence or control over another through coercion, manipulation, or persuasion. This dynamic can be consensual (e.g., in certain BDSM practices) or non-consensual, and it often reflects underlying social, cultural, or psychological factors.

In social hierarchies, dominance/submission dynamics contribute to the establishment and maintenance of status and power relationships within groups or societies. Individuals or groups may compete for dominance or seek to maintain their position within the hierarchy through various means, such as aggression, intimidation, or cooperation.

"Dreams" are experiences of imagined sensations, images, thoughts, and emotions that occur during sleep. They can be vivid and surreal, involving a wide range of content, including memories, fears, desires, and fantasies. Dreams typically occur during the rapid eye movement (REM) stage of sleep, although they can also occur during non-REM sleep stages.

Psychologists and neuroscientists have proposed various theories to explain the function and significance of dreams. These theories suggest that dreams may serve purposes such as processing emotions, consolidating memories, problem-solving, or fulfilling unconscious desires. Additionally, some cultural and spiritual traditions attach symbolic or prophetic meanings to dreams, viewing them as messages from the subconscious or divine realms.

"Dream interpretation" is the process of assigning meaning or significance to the content of dreams. It involves analyzing the symbols, images, emotions, and narratives experienced during sleep in order to gain insight into the dreamer's subconscious mind, emotions, or life circumstances.

Dream interpretation can take various forms, including psychological, cultural, and spiritual approaches. Psychologists may view dreams as reflections of unconscious desires, fears, or unresolved conflicts, using techniques such as free association or dream analysis to uncover underlying meanings. Cultural and spiritual traditions may interpret dreams as messages from the divine, ancestors, or supernatural forces, often relying on symbolic or metaphorical interpretations.

"Economic inequalities" refer to disparities in income, wealth, and access to resources among individuals, households, or groups within a society.
These inequalities can manifest in various forms, including differences in wages and salaries, levels of education, employment opportunities, property ownership, and access to essential services such as healthcare and education.

Economic inequalities are influenced by a variety of factors, including structural and systemic barriers, historical legacies, social policies, and individual circumstances. They can have far-reaching consequences for individuals and communities, contributing to social exclusion, poverty, and intergenerational cycles of disadvantage. Economic inequalities also undermine social cohesion, economic stability, and democratic governance, posing challenges to sustainable development and social progress.

"Consciousness of emotions" refers to the awareness and understanding of one's own emotional experiences. This involves recognizing, interpreting, and managing emotions in oneself and others.

While these two concepts may seem unrelated, they intersect in significant ways. Economic inequalities can impact individuals' emotional well-being, as financial stress, insecurity, and deprivation can lead to negative emotions such as anxiety, frustration, and depression. Additionally, awareness of economic disparities and their impact on society can evoke emotional responses such as empathy, guilt, or anger.

"Empathy"

Refers to the ability to understand and share the feelings, perspectives, and experiences of others. It involves both cognitive and affective components, including the capacity to perceive and comprehend others' emotions, as well as the ability to respond with compassion and care.

Empathy plays a crucial role in interpersonal relationships, social interactions, and moral development. It enables individuals to connect with others on an emotional level, fostering understanding, support, and mutual respect. Empathy also promotes prosocial behaviors such as kindness, cooperation, and altruism, contributing to the well-being and cohesion of communities.

"Entification"

Refers to the cognitive process of treating abstract patterns, concepts, or relationships as if they were tangible entities or "things." It involves attributing properties, intentions, or agency to these abstract constructs, which allows individuals to conceptualize and interact with them more easily.

For example, in everyday language, we often speak of concepts such as "justice," "love," or "the economy" as if they were concrete objects with characteristics and behaviors. This entification allows us to discuss and make sense of complex ideas and phenomena, but it can also lead to misunderstandings or oversimplifications if we fail to recognize their abstract nature.

"Environment" refers to the natural surroundings or external conditions in which living organisms exist and interact. It encompasses both biotic factors (living organisms) and abiotic factors (non-living elements) that shape ecosystems and influence the behavior, growth, and survival of organisms.

The environment includes various components, such as air, water, soil, climate, plants, animals, and microorganisms, as well as human-made structures and influences. These elements interact in complex ways, forming interconnected systems and cycles that sustain life on Earth.

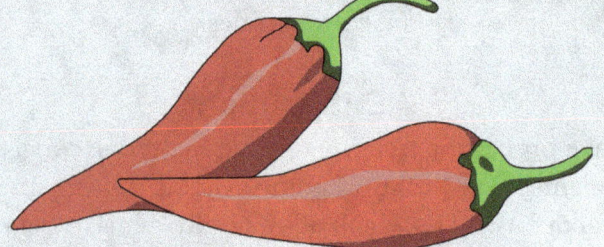

"Envy" is an emotional response characterized by feelings of discontent, resentment, or covetousness towards someone else's possessions, achievements, or qualities. It often arises when individuals perceive others to have something desirable that they lack, leading to feelings of inferiority, bitterness, or hostility.
Envy is a common human emotion that can be triggered by various factors, such as social comparisons, perceived injustices, or personal insecurities. It can manifest in different ways, from subtle jealousy to outright hostility, and may have negative effects on mental well-being, social relationships, and personal satisfaction.

"Etiquette" refers to the set of social conventions, rules, and behaviors that govern polite and respectful interaction in society. It encompasses a wide range of norms and expectations regarding manners, courtesy, and decorum in various social contexts, including everyday interactions, formal gatherings, and professional settings.

Etiquette guides individuals on how to conduct themselves appropriately in different situations, such as how to greet others, engage in conversation, show respect for others' personal space, and navigate social hierarchies. It also includes norms related to table manners, dress codes, gift-giving, and communication etiquette, among others.

Understanding and adhering to etiquette norms is important for fostering positive social interactions, building relationships, and demonstrating respect for others. While etiquette conventions may vary across cultures and contexts, they generally serve to promote harmony, civility, and mutual understanding among individuals and groups.

"Explanation" refers to the act of clarifying or providing information about a topic, event, concept, or phenomenon in order to make it more understandable or comprehensible to others. It involves breaking down complex ideas or processes into simpler terms, providing context, examples, and supporting evidence to help convey meaning and promote understanding.

Explanations can take various forms, including verbal explanations, written descriptions, visual aids, demonstrations, and analogies, depending on the nature of the topic and the preferences of the audience. Effective explanations are clear, concise, and tailored to the needs and prior knowledge of the audience, ensuring that they can grasp the key points and concepts being presented.

"Face" is a concept used in sociology and psychology to describe an individual's public image or self-presentation in social interactions. It represents the social identity that a person seeks to maintain and project to others, often influenced by cultural norms, social expectations, and personal values.

Maintaining "face" involves managing one's reputation, dignity, and social status in various social contexts. This can include preserving one's honor, avoiding embarrassment or loss of credibility, and upholding societal standards of behavior and decorum. Face-saving strategies may involve actions such as apologizing, making excuses, or deflecting criticism to protect one's image and maintain harmony in social relationships.

The concept of face is particularly important in collectivist cultures where social harmony and group cohesion are valued. However, it also applies in individualistic cultures where personal reputation and self-esteem are significant.

- facial communication
- facial expression of anger
- facial expression of contempt
- facial expression of disgust facial expression of fear
- facial expression of happiness
- facial expression of surprise
- facial expressions, masking/modifying of

"Fairness" is a principle that embodies notions of justice, equality, and impartiality in the treatment of individuals or groups. It involves treating all people equitably and without bias, ensuring that everyone has equal opportunities, rights, and access to resources.

Fairness can manifest in various ways, including procedural fairness, distributive fairness, and interpersonal fairness. Procedural fairness refers to the fairness of the processes and procedures used to make decisions, while distributive fairness concerns the fairness of outcomes and resource allocations. Interpersonal fairness relates to the fairness of interpersonal interactions and treatment, such as respect, honesty, and consideration for others.

The concept of fairness is fundamental to social cohesion, cooperation, and trust in societies. It underpins legal systems, social institutions, and ethical frameworks, providing guidelines for resolving conflicts, allocating resources, and promoting the well-being of individuals and communities.

"Folklore" refers to the traditional beliefs, customs, stories, rituals, and practices passed down orally or through cultural expression within a particular community or group. It encompasses a wide range of cultural expressions, including myths, legends, fairy tales, folk songs, proverbs, dances, and rituals, which often reflect the values, beliefs, and experiences of a society.

Folklore serves various functions within communities, such as preserving cultural heritage, transmitting knowledge and wisdom, reinforcing social norms and identities, and providing entertainment and communal bonding. It is often deeply intertwined with local landscapes, environments, and historical contexts, shaping people's understanding of themselves, their place in the world, and their relationships with others. Exploring folklore can provide insights into the cultural diversity and richness of human societies. By examining folk traditions, narratives, and practices from different cultures and regions, readers can gain a deeper understanding of the shared human experiences, values, and concerns that underpin folklore traditions worldwide. Additionally, discussing the role of folklore in shaping collective memory, identity formation, and social cohesion can inspire readers to appreciate and celebrate the diverse cultural expressions that enrich our global heritage.

"Family" is a fundamental social institution that typically consists of individuals related by blood, marriage, adoption, or close emotional bonds. Families play a central role in shaping the identities, values, and experiences of their members, providing emotional support, socialization, and caregiving throughout the life course.

Families vary widely in structure, composition, and dynamics across cultures and societies. While the nuclear family (parents and children) is a common form, other arrangements such as extended families, single-parent families, blended families, and chosen families also exist. Additionally, families may vary in size, roles, and functions based on cultural, socioeconomic, and historical factors. Family relationships are characterized by intimacy, interdependence, and reciprocity, with members sharing responsibilities, resources, and experiences. Families fulfill various functions, including providing emotional support, socialization, economic assistance, and caregiving for children, elderly relatives, and individuals with disabilities.

"Father" and "mother" are familial roles traditionally associated with parents who provide care, guidance, and support to their children within a family unit. These roles are often defined by biological parenthood, but they can also be fulfilled through adoption, step-parenting, or other forms of guardianship.

Fathers and mothers typically play complementary roles within the family, each contributing to the emotional, physical, and social development of their children in unique ways. Fathers may be associated with providing protection, discipline, and financial support, while mothers are often associated with nurturing, caregiving, and emotional support. However, these roles are not strictly determined by gender, and individuals may fulfill parental responsibilities in a variety of ways based on their abilities, circumstances, and cultural norms.

"Fear" is an emotional response characterized by feelings of apprehension, anxiety, or distress in the face of perceived danger, threat, or uncertainty. It is a natural and adaptive reaction that helps individuals recognize and respond to potential risks or harm in their environment.

Fears can be triggered by a wide range of stimuli, including physical dangers, social situations, perceived failures, or existential threats. Common fears include fear of heights, fear of public speaking, fear of failure, fear of rejection, fear of death, and fear of the unknown. Fears can vary in intensity and duration, ranging from mild discomfort to overwhelming panic. While fear can be protective and motivating, excessive or irrational fears can interfere with daily functioning and quality of life, leading to avoidance behaviors, phobias, or anxiety disorders. Overcoming fears often involves facing them gradually, learning coping strategies, and seeking support from others.

The fear of death, known as **"thanatophobia"**, is a common existential fear that stems from the awareness of one's mortality and the uncertainty of what happens after death. It is a deeply ingrained fear in human psychology and can provoke intense anxiety and existential distress.

Overcoming the fear of death can be a challenging and deeply personal journey. While it may not be possible to completely eliminate this fear, individuals can develop coping mechanisms and perspectives that help them manage their fear and find peace. One approach to overcoming the fear of death is through existential therapy or philosophical reflection, which involves exploring the meaning of life, one's values, and beliefs about death and the afterlife. This process can help individuals come to terms with their mortality and find a sense of purpose and acceptance in the face of death. Spiritual or religious beliefs can also provide comfort and solace in coping with the fear of death. Belief in an afterlife or a higher power can offer reassurance and a sense of continuity beyond physical existence.

"Food preferences" refer to the individual or cultural inclinations towards certain types of foods over others. These preferences are shaped by a variety of factors, including biological, psychological, cultural, social, and environmental influences.

Biological factors such as genetics, taste sensitivity, and physiological responses to certain foods can influence food preferences. For example, some individuals may have a genetic predisposition to prefer sweet or savory flavors, while others may be more sensitive to bitter tastes.

Psychological factors, such as past experiences, memories, and emotions associated with particular foods, can also shape preferences. Comfort foods, for example, are often chosen for their emotional associations and ability to provide a sense of comfort or nostalgia.

Cultural and social factors play a significant role in shaping food preferences as well. Cultural traditions, customs, and rituals surrounding food can influence what is considered acceptable or desirable to eat within a particular community. Additionally, social influences such as peer pressure, media, advertising, and social norms can impact food choices and preferences.

Environmental factors, such as food availability, accessibility, affordability, and convenience, also influence food preferences. Individuals may be more likely to choose foods that are readily available, affordable, and easy to prepare.

Karolina Grabowska

"Food sharing" is a social practice that involves the distribution and consumption of food among individuals or groups within a community. It is a universal human behavior with deep cultural and social significance, serving various functions beyond simple sustenance.

Food sharing has been integral to human survival and cooperation throughout history, facilitating bonding, reciprocity, and social cohesion within groups. It fosters relationships, strengthens social ties, and reinforces solidarity among individuals and communities.

Food sharing occurs in various forms, including communal meals, potlucks, feasts, and food exchanges. It may take place within families, among friends, during cultural or religious celebrations, or as part of larger social events and gatherings.

Beyond its social functions, food sharing also plays a role in addressing food insecurity, reducing waste, and promoting sustainability. Sharing excess food with those in need helps alleviate hunger and food insecurity, while redistributing surplus food reduces food waste and contributes to environmental conservation efforts.

"Generosity" is the quality of being kind, selfless, and willing to give or share resources, time, or assistance with others without expecting anything in return. It involves acts of giving freely and willingly, whether it's material possessions, emotional support, or acts of kindness.

Generosity is a fundamental aspect of human nature that fosters compassion, empathy, and social connection. It can take many forms, from small gestures of kindness to significant acts of philanthropy. Regardless of scale, generosity enriches both the giver and the recipient, strengthening bonds within communities and fostering a sense of interconnectedness. Practicing generosity can have profound benefits for individuals and society as a whole.

"Attempts to predict the future"

Throughout history, humans have tried various methods to predict the future, from ancient practices like astrology and divination to modern statistical analysis and futurology. While these methods offer insights and help in planning, the future remains uncertain due to its complexity and unpredictability. Exploring the history and approaches to prediction can deepen our understanding of human efforts to anticipate what lies ahead and the challenges inherent in doing so. It also underscores the importance of resilience and adaptability in navigating uncertainty.

"Gestures" are non-verbal actions that convey meaning, emotions, or intentions. They include emblematic gestures with specific meanings, illustrative gestures that accompany speech, descriptive gestures that depict actions, regulatory gestures for turn-taking, and affective gestures for expressing emotions. Understanding gestures is essential for effective communication, as they provide additional context and convey social cues. In your book, exploring the role of gestures can help readers improve their communication skills and navigate diverse cultural contexts with sensitivity and understanding.

"Gift giving" is a universal practice that involves exchanging items or gestures as a symbol of goodwill or celebration. It serves to express gratitude, mark special occasions, demonstrate generosity, and foster relationships. Gifts can be tangible items or intangible experiences, and they play a significant role in social bonding and reciprocity. Exploring gift giving in your book can provide insights into human relationships and culture, inspiring readers to cultivate generosity and meaningful connections in their lives.

"Distinguishing between **'good' and 'bad'**" involves evaluating actions, behaviors, or outcomes based on moral, ethical, or societal norms to determine their perceived value or quality.

"Good" typically refers to actions or behaviors that are considered beneficial, virtuous, or morally upright according to prevailing standards or values. Examples of "good" actions may include acts of kindness, honesty, compassion, and generosity.

On the other hand, "bad" refers to actions or behaviors that are perceived as harmful, immoral, or negative in nature. Examples of "bad" actions may include acts of dishonesty, cruelty, selfishness, and injustice.

The distinction between "good" and "bad" is subjective and can vary depending on cultural, religious, and individual perspectives. What may be considered "good" in one context or culture may be viewed differently in another.

Mohamed Hassan

"Gossip" is the informal sharing of information about others, often focusing on personal or scandalous details. While it can serve as a means of social bonding and exchanging news, gossip can also harm relationships and spread misinformation. Exploring gossip in your book can shed light on social dynamics and communication patterns, helping readers navigate its complexities with sensitivity and integrity.

"Government" refers to the system responsible for governing a country or community. It includes making laws (legislative), enforcing them (executive), and interpreting them (judicial). Governments vary in form, such as democracy or monarchy, and are shaped by cultural and historical factors. Exploring government in your book can help readers understand governance, democracy, and civic engagement.

"Grammar" refers to the system of rules and principles governing the structure, composition, and usage of language. It encompasses syntax (sentence structure), morphology (word formation), semantics (meaning), and phonology (sound patterns), among other aspects.

Understanding grammar is essential for effective communication, as it provides the framework for constructing clear and coherent sentences, conveying meaning accurately, and following conventions that ensure clarity and precision in language use. Grammar can be studied and taught at various levels, from basic rules of sentence construction to more advanced principles of syntax and semantics. It is taught in schools as part of language education and is also studied in fields such as linguistics, communication, and writing.

"Group living" refers to the social arrangement where individuals of the same species reside and interact together. It serves several purposes, including protection, resource acquisition, social interaction, reproductive success, and division of labor.
This phenomenon is observed across various species, including humans, and facilitates cooperation, communication, and mutual support. Exploring group living in your book can provide insights into social behavior, cooperation, and adaptation. It highlights the benefits and challenges of living in groups and their implications for individuals and societies.

Embracing the World | 45

"Habituation" is a psychological process where an organism becomes accustomed to a stimulus after repeated exposure, leading to a decreased response over time. Essentially, it's the tendency
to get used to something and pay less attention to it as it becomes familiar. This process allows organisms to conserve energy and focus attention on new or important stimuli instead. Habituation is observed in various organisms, from simple organisms like single-celled organisms to complex animals like humans. It plays a crucial role in learning, memory, and adaptation to

"Healing the sick" refers to the process of providing care and treatment to individuals who are ill or injured with the goal of restoring their health and well-being. It encompasses various medical interventions, therapies, and practices aimed at alleviating symptoms, curing diseases, and promoting recovery.

Healing the sick can involve a range of healthcare professionals, including doctors, nurses, therapists, and other caregivers, who work collaboratively to diagnose, treat, and manage patients' conditions. It may also involve complementary and alternative therapies, such as acupuncture, herbal medicine, or spiritual practices, depending on cultural and individual preferences.

"Hope" is a powerful and positive emotion that arises from the belief in the possibility of a better future, despite present challenges or adversity. It is characterized by optimism, resilience, and a sense of possibility, even in the face of uncertainty or hardship.

Hope motivates individuals to persevere, pursue goals, and overcome obstacles in pursuit of a desired outcome. It provides strength and resilience during difficult times, inspiring perseverance and determination in the face of adversity. Hope is not merely wishful thinking or passive optimism; it involves taking action and making efforts to create positive change. It fuels creativity, problem-solving, and adaptive coping strategies, empowering individuals to navigate challenges and work towards a brighter future.

"Hospitality" refers to the practice of welcoming, hosting, and providing care for guests or visitors in a generous and warm manner. It involves offering hospitality in various settings, such as homes, hotels, restaurants, and other establishments, with the aim of creating a comfortable and inviting environment for guests.

Hospitality encompasses several key elements:

Warm Welcome: Hospitality begins with a friendly and genuine welcome extended to guests upon their arrival. This sets the tone for the interaction and creates a positive first impression.

Comfort and Care: Hospitality involves ensuring the comfort and well-being of guests during their stay or visit. This may include providing amenities, catering to individual needs, and offering assistance or support as needed.

Generosity and Generosity: Hospitality is characterized by generosity and generosity towards guests, whether it's through offering food and drinks, providing accommodations, or extending other acts of kindness and hospitality.

Respect and Consideration: Hospitality entails treating guests with respect, dignity, and consideration, regardless of their background, preferences, or circumstances. It involves listening attentively, being responsive to guests' needs, and maintaining professionalism at all times.

Creating Memorable Experiences: Hospitality aims to create memorable and enjoyable experiences for guests, leaving them feeling valued, appreciated, and cared for. This involves paying attention to details, anticipating needs, and going above and beyond to exceed expectations.

"Hygienic care" refers to practices and habits aimed at maintaining cleanliness and promoting health and well-being. It encompasses a range of activities focused on personal and environmental hygiene to prevent the spread of illness, infection, and disease.

Hygienic care includes:

Personal Hygiene: This involves practices such as regular bathing or showering, washing hands frequently, brushing teeth, and grooming hair. Personal hygiene helps to remove dirt, sweat, and bacteria from the body, reducing the risk of infection and promoting overall cleanliness.

Dental Hygiene: Good dental hygiene includes brushing teeth regularly, flossing, and visiting the dentist for check-ups and cleanings. Proper dental care helps to prevent tooth decay, gum disease, and other oral health issues.

Hand Hygiene: Washing hands with soap and water or using hand sanitizer is essential for preventing the spread of germs and bacteria, especially before eating, after using the restroom, or after coughing or sneezing.

Food Hygiene: Practicing food hygiene involves handling, preparing, and storing food safely to prevent contamination and foodborne illnesses. This includes washing fruits and vegetables, cooking meat thoroughly, and storing food at the correct temperatures.

Environmental Hygiene: Keeping living spaces, work environments, and public areas clean and sanitized helps to reduce the risk of illness and promote overall health. This includes regular cleaning of surfaces, disinfecting high-touch areas, and proper waste disposal.

Hygienic care is essential for maintaining health and preventing the spread of infectious diseases, particularly in settings such as hospitals, schools, and public spaces. By adopting hygienic practices as part of daily routines, individuals can protect themselves and others wfrom illness and contribute to a cleaner and healthier environment.

Karolina Grabowska

"Collective Identity" refers to the shared sense of belonging, values, beliefs, and experiences that unite individuals as part of a larger group or community. It encompasses the collective consciousness, cultural heritage, and social bonds that shape the identity of a group and influence its members' sense of self.

Key aspects of collective identity include:

- *Shared Beliefs and Values:* Collective identity is often rooted in shared beliefs, values, and ideologies that members of a group uphold and adhere to. These may include religious beliefs, political ideologies, cultural norms, or social ideals that define the group's identity and shape its worldview.
- *Cultural and Ethnic Heritage:* Cultural and ethnic identity play a significant role in shaping collective identity, as they encompass shared traditions, customs, language, and history that contribute to a group's sense of identity and belonging.
- *Shared Experiences and History:* Collective identity is influenced by shared experiences, historical events, and collective memories that bind group members together and shape their identity over time. These may include triumphs, struggles, or challenges that the group has faced collectively
- *Group Membership and Social Identity:* Group membership and social identity are central to collective identity, as individuals identify with and define themselves in relation to the groups they belong to, whether it's based on race, ethnicity, nationality, religion, gender, or other social categories.
- *Collective Action and Solidarity:* Collective identity often fosters a sense of solidarity and collective action among group members, as they come together to pursue common goals, advocate for shared interests, or address collective challenges.

Collective identity can manifest in various forms, including national identity, ethnic identity, religious identity, political identity, or identity based on shared interests or affiliations. It shapes social interactions, influences behavior, and plays a significant role in shaping individual and group identities.

"Unthinkable or Tabooed" refers to topics, ideas, or behaviors considered socially unacceptable or culturally sensitive. These subjects, like sexuality, religion, death, mental health, or politics, are often avoided due to potential offense or discomfort. Exploring taboo topics can deepen understanding of cultural norms and societal boundaries. In your book, addressing taboos with sensitivity can spark important conversations and promote social awareness.

"Imagery" is the use of descriptive language to create vivid mental pictures or sensory experiences. It appeals to the senses—sight, sound, taste, touch, and smell—to enhance writing and engage readers. Through visual, auditory, olfactory, gustatory, and tactile descriptions, imagery brings scenes to life, evokes emotions, and makes writing more memorable and immersive. In your book, exploring imagery can enrich your writing and captivate readers by creating vivid mental images and sensory experiences.

"In-group distinguished from out-group" refers to how individuals categorize themselves and others into groups. The "in-group" is the group they belong to, while the "out-group" is perceived as different. This categorization can lead to favoritism towards the in-group and prejudice towards the out-group, contributing to social tensions and conflict. Understanding these dynamics helps in comprehending social identity and intergroup relations. In your book, exploring these distinctions can provide insights into group behavior and strategies for promoting empathy and cooperation between groups.

"In-group biases in favor of" refers to the tendency for individuals to favor members of their own group. This bias leads to positive attitudes, preferences, and cooperative behavior towards the in-group, while often resulting in discrimination against out-group members. Understanding these biases is crucial for addressing prejudice and promoting inclusivity. In your book, exploring in-group biases can provide insights into group dynamics and strategies for fostering positive intergroup relations.

"Inheritance rules"

Determine how assets are distributed after someone's death. They include intestacy laws for those without a will, testamentary wills for those with one, cultural and religious practices, legal frameworks, and evolving norms. Understanding these rules is important for estate planning and ensuring assets are distributed according to one's wishes. In your book, exploring inheritance rules can provide insights into legal, cultural, and ethical considerations, empowering readers to make informed decisions about their estates and legacy planning.

"Institutions"

Organized systems that regulate social behavior and facilitate collective activities within a society. They include formal structures like government bodies, educational institutions, corporations, and cultural organizations. Institutions fulfill essential social functions, such as governance, education, healthcare, economic exchange, and cultural expression. They possess authority and power to enforce rules and make decisions, adapting and evolving over time to meet changing societal needs. Understanding institutions is crucial for comprehending social organization, power dynamics, and mechanisms of social change. In your book, exploring institutions can provide insights into their role in shaping individuals' lives and societal development, inspiring readers to advocate for positive institutional change.

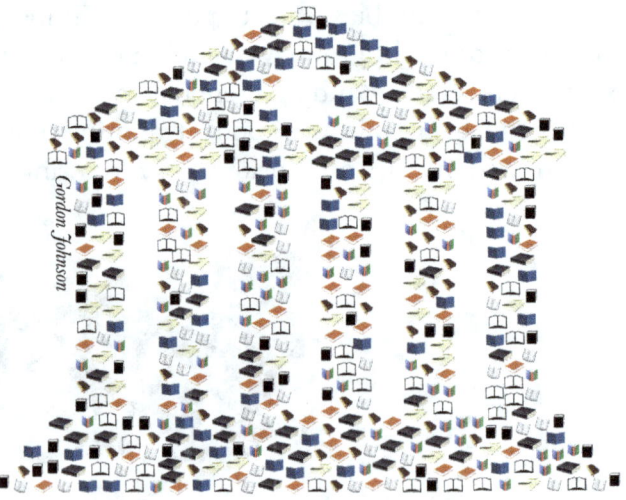

"Insulting" refers to offensive behavior or language aimed at causing harm or offense to someone. It often involves verbal abuse, personal attacks, and intent to harm. Insults damage relationships and erode trust. Addressing insulting behavior requires promoting respect and constructive communication. In your book, discussing strategies for fostering respectful interactions can empower readers to navigate interpersonal challenges with dignity and integrity.

"Intention" refers to the purpose behind a person's actions or behaviors. It involves a conscious decision to pursue a specific goal or outcome, driven by underlying motivations and values. Understanding intentions helps interpret human behavior and decision-making. In your book, exploring intentions can provide insights into the factors influencing actions and fostering self-awareness and purposeful action.

"Interest in Bioforms" refers to curiosity about living organisms or entities resembling them. People are drawn to bioforms for scientific exploration, aesthetic appreciation, ecological awareness, and philosophical reflection. This interest can inspire innovation and promote ecological stewardship. In your book, exploring interest in bioforms can foster appreciation for biodiversity and the interconnectedness of life.

"Interpolation" is a mathematical technique used to estimate values between known data points. It involves constructing a function that passes through the given data points, allowing for the estimation of values at intermediate points within the range of the data. This method is commonly used in various fields such as computer graphics, signal processing, and numerical analysis.

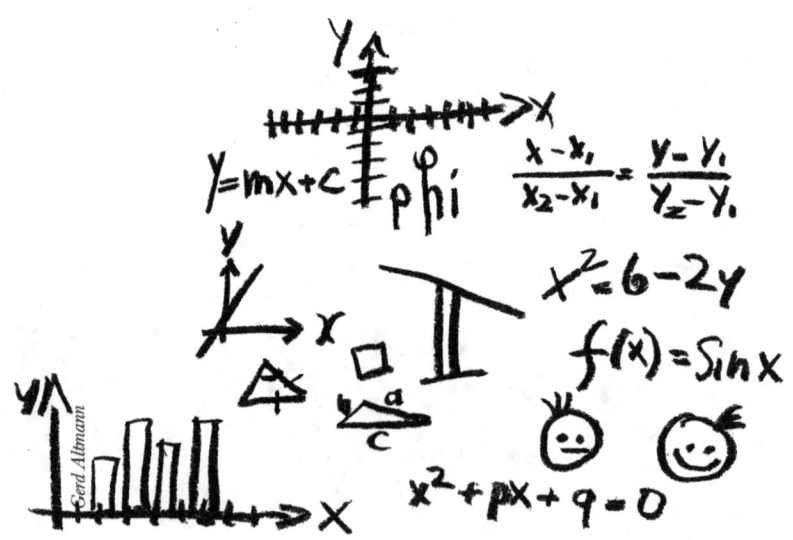

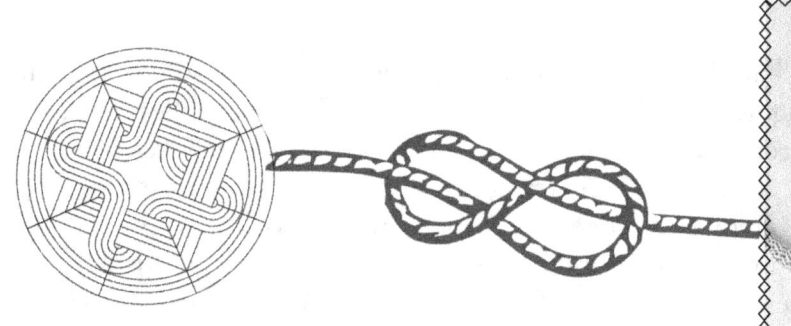

"Interpreting Behavior" involves analyzing and understanding the actions, gestures, and expressions of individuals or groups to infer their thoughts, feelings, intentions, or motivations. This process often involves considering contextual factors, cultural norms, and psychological theories to make sense of observed behaviors. It's essential in fields such as psychology, sociology, and anthropology for understanding human interactions and societal dynamics.

"Intertwining" refers to the act of twisting or weaving things together, creating a complex and interconnected structure.
It can be used metaphorically to describe the blending or merging of different elements, ideas, or concepts, resulting in a cohesive and interconnected whole. This term is often used in literature, art, and discussions about complex relationships or interconnected systems.

"Jokes" are humorous statements, actions, or situations designed to evoke laughter or amusement. They often involve wordplay, irony, satire, or unexpected twists in order to entertain an audience. Jokes serve various purposes, such as breaking tension, conveying cultural norms, or simply providing enjoyment. They are a common form of social interaction and communication, found in everyday conversations, performances, and written media.

"Judging" others involves forming opinions or making evaluations about individuals based on their actions, behaviors, or characteristics. While it's natural for humans to make judgments as part of their cognitive processes, it's important to be aware of biases and prejudices that may influence these judgments unfairly. Practicing empathy, understanding context, and recognizing individual complexities can help mitigate the negative effects of judgmental behavior and foster more compassionate interactions.

"Kin" typically refers to one's family or relatives, including blood relations and sometimes extended family members. It can also refer to a group of people with shared characteristics, interests, or goals, such as a community or tribe. The concept of kinship is fundamental to human societies, shaping social structures, roles, and relationships. It encompasses bonds of affection, support, and responsibility, playing a significant role in personal identity and cultural traditions.

"Language" is a system of communication consisting of symbols, sounds, gestures, or written characters used to convey meaning and express thoughts, ideas, and emotions. It serves as a primary means for humans to interact, share knowledge, and preserve culture. Languages vary widely across different regions and cultures, with thousands of distinct languages spoken worldwide. Studying language involves examining its structure, grammar, semantics, and pragmatics, as well as its social and cultural contexts. Language acquisition, evolution, and diversity are topics of interest in fields such as linguistics, psychology, and anthropology.

"Law" refers to a system of rules, regulations, and principles established by a governing authority to regulate behavior within a society and enforce justice. It encompasses various branches, including criminal law, civil law, administrative law, and international law, each serving specific purposes and addressing different aspects of human interaction. The legal system provides mechanisms for resolving disputes, protecting individual rights, and maintaining order. It also reflects cultural values, societal norms, and evolving standards of justice. Studying law involves understanding legal concepts, precedents, statutes, and case law, as well as legal reasoning and interpretation.

A **"Leader"** is someone who guides, inspires, and influences others towards a common goal or purpose. Leadership involves possessing qualities such as vision, integrity, empathy, decisiveness, and the ability to communicate effectively. Leaders can emerge in various contexts, including politics, business, academia, and community organizations. They provide direction, motivation, and support to their followers, fostering collaboration and achieving collective objectives. Effective leadership is essential for driving innovation, fostering positive change, and building cohesive and successful teams or communities.

A **"Lever"** is a simple machine consisting of a rigid bar or beam that pivots around a fixed point, called a fulcrum. It's used to amplify force or change the direction of applied force. Levers are categorized into three types based on the relative positions of the fulcrum, the effort (applied force), and the load (the resistance being moved): first-class, second-class, and third-class levers. Levers are widely used in various applications, from basic tools like seesaws and crowbars to complex mechanical systems in engineering and machinery. They operate based on the principle of torque, enabling humans to perform tasks more efficiently and with less effort.

"Likes and Dislikes" refer to preferences or attitudes towards specific things, experiences, or activities. Likes are things that individuals enjoy, find appealing, or derive pleasure from, while dislikes are things they find unappealing, unpleasant, or undesirable. These preferences can vary greatly among individuals and may be influenced by factors such as personal tastes, cultural background, past experiences, and social influences. Understanding one's likes and dislikes can help inform decision-making, shape personal identity, and contribute to overall well-being and satisfaction.

"Linguistic Redundancy" refers to the use of unnecessary or repetitive language in communication. It occurs when information is conveyed in a way that includes more words or elements than needed to express the intended meaning. While some degree of redundancy can enhance clarity and reinforce understanding, excessive redundancy can lead to verbosity and inefficiency in communication. Linguistic redundancy is often observed in spoken language, where speakers may repeat themselves or use filler words and phrases. However, it can also occur in written language through the use of redundant modifiers, qualifiers, or redundant expressions. Effective communication aims to strike a balance between clarity and conciseness, minimizing redundancy while ensuring the message is conveyed accurately and comprehensively.

"Logical Notions" are fundamental concepts in logic that serve as the building blocks for reasoning and inference. They include principles such as identity, non-contradiction, excluded middle, implication, and negation. These notions provide the framework for evaluating the validity of arguments, making deductions, and drawing conclusions based on premises. For example, the law of non-contradiction states that a statement cannot be both true and false at the same time and in the same sense. Logical notions are essential for understanding and analyzing logical arguments, both in formal logic and in everyday reasoning.

- logical notion of "and"
- logical notion of "equivalent"
- logical notion of "general/particular"
- logical notion of "not"
- logical notion of "opposite"
- logical notion of "part/whole"
- logical notion of "same"

Adrian Eyre

"And": In logic, "and" is a logical connective used to combine two statements. It indicates that both statements must be true for the combined statement to be true. For example, "It is raining AND the streets are wet" is true only if both conditions are met.

"Equivalent": In logic, "equivalent" refers to two statements or propositions that have the same truth value. If two statements are equivalent, they are either both true or both false. For example, "It is raining" is equivalent to "The streets are wet" if both statements are true, or if both are false.

"General/Particular": This logical notion relates to the distinction between general statements, which apply to a whole class or category, and particular statements, which refer to specific instances within that class. For example, "All cats have fur" is a general statement, while "My cat has fur" is a particular statement.

"Not": In logic, "not" is a negation operator used to reverse the truth value of a statement. If a statement is true, its negation is false, and vice versa. For example, the negation of "It is raining" is "It is not raining."

"Opposite": In logic, "opposite" refers to two statements or concepts that are mutually exclusive or contradictory. The opposite of a true statement is a false statement, and vice versa. For example, the opposite of "It is raining" is "It is not raining."

"Part/Whole": This logical notion describes the relationship between a part and the whole of which it is a component. A part is a subset or component of the whole, and the whole encompasses all of its parts. For example, "The wheels are part of the car" illustrates the part/whole relationship.

"Same": In logic, "same" indicates identity or equality between two objects or concepts. If two things are the same, they are identical or indistinguishable from each other. For example, "The morning star is the same as the evening star" expresses the identity of two celestial objects (Venus).

"Magic"

Refers to the practice of using supernatural or mystical abilities, rituals, or spells to influence events or outcomes beyond natural laws or human abilities. It encompasses a wide range of beliefs, practices, and traditions found in various cultures throughout history. Magic often involves invoking spiritual forces, deities, or supernatural entities to achieve desired effects, such as healing, divination, protection, or manipulation of the natural world. While magic is often associated with folklore, mythology, and fantasy, it has also been an integral part of religious and spiritual practices in many cultures. Additionally, stage magic, also known as illusionism or conjuring, involves performing tricks and sleight of hand to create the illusion of supernatural feats for entertainment purposes.

Magic to Increase Life: Rituals or spells to extend lifespan or vitality, drawing from folklore and mythology.

Magic to Sustain Life: Practices to preserve health and well-being, including fertility, healing, and protection.

Magic to Win Love: Rituals or spells aimed at attracting romantic affection, often invoking love deities or using charms.

Regarding the merit, beliefs in magical practices vary greatly among individuals and cultures. While some may find personal meaning or solace in these practices, it's essential to approach them with critical thinking and ethical considerations. There's value in understanding the cultural significance and symbolism behind such beliefs, even if one does not personally subscribe to them.

"Making Comparisons" involves evaluating similarities and differences between two or more things, concepts, or situations. It's a fundamental cognitive process used to analyze, understand, and communicate information. Comparisons can be made based on various criteria such as size, shape, color, function, effectiveness, or quality. They help individuals make decisions, form opinions, and gain insights by highlighting patterns, trends, or contrasts. Whether comparing products, ideas, cultures, or experiences, this process allows for deeper understanding and informed decision-making.

"Traditional Male and Female Roles"

typically adhere to societal norms and expectations based on biological sex. In traditional societies, these roles often reinforce stereotypical attributes and behaviors associated with masculinity and femininity.

Traditional male roles often include being the primary breadwinner, displaying strength, assertiveness, and leadership qualities. Men are expected to take on responsibilities outside the home, such as providing financial support, making decisions, and engaging in physically demanding tasks.

On the other hand, traditional female roles typically revolve around caregiving, nurturing, and maintaining the household. Women are often expected to prioritize family and domestic duties, such as cooking, cleaning, and childcare. They may also be encouraged to embody traits such as empathy, sensitivity, and emotional expressiveness.

These traditional roles have been shaped by cultural norms, religious beliefs, and historical practices, and they have been perpetuated through socialization processes within families, educational institutions, and media representations. However, it's important to recognize that these roles are not universally applicable, and individuals may deviate from or challenge them based on personal beliefs, societal changes, and evolving understandings of gender.

"Traditional Gender Roles" are societal expectations and norms that dictate the behaviors, roles, and responsibilities considered appropriate for individuals based on their gender. These roles have typically been based on binary understandings of gender, with men and women expected to conform to stereotypical characteristics and behaviors. For example, traditional gender roles may dictate that men should be the primary breadwinners, assertive, and dominant, while women should be caregivers, nurturing, and submissive. These roles have been reinforced through cultural traditions, religious beliefs, and social institutions, such as marriage and family structures.

In contrast, modern gender roles are evolving and less rigidly defined, reflecting a broader understanding of gender diversity and equality. Modern gender roles recognize that gender identity is not limited to a binary framework and that individuals may identify outside of traditional male and female categories. As a result, modern gender roles encourage greater flexibility, inclusivity, and acceptance of diverse expressions of gender identity and behavior. For example, modern gender roles may embrace men who are involved in caregiving and domestic responsibilities or women who pursue careers traditionally dominated by men.

Overall, while traditional gender roles are rooted in historical and cultural contexts and tend to reinforce gender stereotypes and inequalities, modern gender roles strive to promote gender equality, inclusivity, and the recognition of individual autonomy and agency regardless of gender identity.

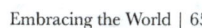

Maiconfz
Оксана Марчук

"Social Relations Manipulating" is to intentionally influence or control the dynamics, interactions, or perceptions within a social group or between individuals for personal gain or a specific agenda. This manipulation can take various forms, such as:

- **Deception:** Misrepresenting information or concealing intentions to sway opinions or actions.
- **Persuasion:** Using tactics such as flattery, coercion, or emotional appeals to convince others to act in a certain way.
- **Power Dynamics:** Leveraging one's position or authority to assert dominance or influence decision-making processes.
- **Social Engineering:** Orchestrating situations or environments to shape social behaviors or outcomes.
- **Gaslighting:** Manipulating someone's perception of reality to undermine their confidence or control over a situation.
- **Social Isolation:** Deliberately excluding or ostracizing individuals to weaken their social connections or influence.
- **Propaganda:** Disseminating biased or misleading information to shape public opinion or attitudes towards certain groups or ideas.

While manipulation of social relations can be used for both positive and negative purposes, it often raises ethical concerns about honesty, autonomy, and fairness. It's important to be mindful of the intentions and consequences of such manipulation and to prioritize respectful and ethical interactions in social contexts.

"Marriage" is a social and legal institution that formalizes the union between two individuals, typically with the intent of establishing a long-term partnership, often involving shared responsibilities, rights, and obligations. While the specific customs and ceremonies surrounding marriage vary widely across cultures and religions, common elements often include vows or promises exchanged between partners, the presence of witnesses, and the recognition of the union by the community or governing authorities.

Marriage serves various purposes, including:

Emotional and Social Bonding: Marriage provides a framework for emotional intimacy, companionship, and mutual support between partners. It creates a sense of belonging and connection within families and communities.

Legal and Economic Benefits: Marriage often confers legal rights and benefits to spouses, such as inheritance rights, access to healthcare and insurance, tax advantages, and eligibility for spousal benefits and protections under the law.

Family and Reproductive Purposes: Marriage traditionally serves as the foundation for starting a family and raising children. It provides a stable environment for child-rearing and contributes to the continuity of family lineage and cultural traditions.

Social and Religious Significance: Marriage is often imbued with cultural, religious, or spiritual significance, symbolizing commitments, values, and beliefs shared by the couple and their community.

While marriage is widely practiced and valued in many societies, attitudes and norms surrounding marriage have evolved over time, reflecting changing social, cultural, and legal contexts. Additionally, there is increasing recognition of diverse forms of partnerships and family structures beyond traditional marital arrangements, including civil unions, domestic partnerships, and same-sex marriages, reflecting efforts to promote equality and inclusivity in society.

Laura Tancredi

"Materialism" is a philosophical worldview or belief system that emphasizes the primacy of physical matter and the material world over non-material or spiritual aspects of existence. In materialism, reality is seen as fundamentally consisting of physical entities and processes, with no supernatural or metaphysical dimensions.

In its philosophical sense, materialism can manifest in various forms:

Metaphysical Materialism: This perspective holds that everything that exists is composed of material substances or physical matter, and all phenomena can be explained by the interactions of matter and energy according to natural laws.

Economic Materialism: In this context, materialism refers to a focus on material possessions, wealth, and consumerism as primary sources of value and happiness. This perspective often prioritizes material wealth and possessions over spiritual or emotional fulfillment.

Scientific Materialism: This viewpoint emphasizes the importance of empirical evidence and scientific methodology in understanding the natural world. Scientific materialists believe that knowledge should be derived from observable phenomena and testable hypotheses, rather than relying on metaphysical or supernatural explanations.

While materialism can provide valuable insights into the physical universe and drive technological advancements, critics argue that excessive materialism can lead to shallow values, environmental degradation, and social inequalities. Additionally, materialism may overlook or devalue subjective experiences, emotions, and spiritual dimensions of human existence, leading to a sense of emptiness or disillusionment despite material wealth and possessions.

"Measuring" refers to the process of determining the quantity, size, or extent of something using a standard unit of measurement. This process involves comparing an unknown quantity to a known reference or standard in order to express it numerically. Measuring is essential in various fields such as science, engineering, construction, commerce, and everyday life.

Units of measurement are used to quantify different attributes, such as length, mass, volume, time, temperature, and many others. Examples of commonly used units include meters, kilograms, liters, seconds, degrees Celsius, and so on. These units provide a standardized way to communicate and compare measurements across different contexts and locations. While many units of measurement are standardized and widely used internationally (e.g., the metric system), it's important to note that there are also non-universal units that vary based on cultural, historical, or regional factors. For example, the United States commonly uses the imperial system for measurements such as feet, pounds, and gallons, while other countries primarily use the metric system. This variation can sometimes lead to confusion or inefficiencies when communicating measurements across different regions or disciplines.

"Memor" is the process of encoding, storing, and retrieving information. It comes in different types:

Sensory Memory: Holds brief sensory input.
Short-term Memory: Temporarily stores information.
Long-term Memory: Stores information for an extended period.
Explicit Memory: Conscious recollection of facts and events.
Implicit Memory: Unconscious memory influencing behavior.

Memory is influenced by attention, rehearsal, and emotional arousal. Understanding memory helps with learning, diagnosing memory disorders, and improving memory techniques.

A **"Melody"** is a sequence of musical tones or pitches arranged in a coherent and pleasing manner. It is the main or principal musical line in a piece of music that carries the tune or theme. Melodies are characterized by their contour (the shape of the pitches over time), rhythm (the arrangement of durations and accents), and intervallic structure (the distance between successive pitches).

Melodies often serve as the focal point of a musical composition, providing a memorable and expressive element that listeners can follow and identify. They can be sung by a vocalist or played on a musical instrument, and they can vary widely in complexity and style depending on the genre, cultural context, and composer's intent.

Melodies are an essential component of music, conveying emotion, narrative, and artistic expression. They can evoke a wide range of feelings and moods, from joy and excitement to sadness and nostalgia. Additionally, melodies can interact with other musical elements such as harmony, rhythm, and texture to create rich and layered musical experiences.

Rahul Yadav

"Music" is an art form that uses sound to convey emotion and meaning.
It includes elements like melody, harmony, rhythm, and timbre. Music is universal, crossing cultural and linguistic boundaries, and plays a significant role in entertainment, cultural identity, and emotional expression. It can be experienced in various settings and has therapeutic applications. Overall, music enriches the human experience and fosters connections between people.

"Rhythm" is the organized pattern of beats or movements that create tempo and structure in music, dance, or poetry. It involves the repetition of stressed and unstressed elements, enhancing expression and communication.

Aquib Azad

"Mental Maps" are cognitive representations of physical spaces created in the mind. They help individuals navigate and understand their surroundings by providing spatial awareness, topographical information, and landmarks. These maps are subjective and influenced by personal experiences. Mental maps are crucial for navigation and understanding environments, aiding in everyday tasks and informing urban planning and design.

"Mentalese" is a theoretical idea proposing a universal mental language underlying human thought. It suggests that thoughts are represented in the mind using a language-like system of symbols, facilitating cognitive processes like problem-solving and language acquisition. While influential, its existence and nature remain debated in cognitive science and philosophy.

Gerd Altmann

A **"Metaphor"** is a figure of speech that draws a comparison between two unrelated things by stating that one thing is another. Unlike similes, which use "like" or "as" to make comparisons, metaphors assert a direct equivalence. For example, "Time is a thief" or "Her eyes were sparkling diamonds." Metaphors are used to convey complex ideas, emotions, or experiences by linking them to more familiar or concrete concepts, enriching language and stimulating imagination. They can be found in literature, poetry, everyday language, and even in visual art and music. Metaphors help us understand abstract concepts by framing them in terms of more tangible experiences, facilitating communication and enhancing expression.

A **"Metonym"** is a figure of speech in which one word or phrase is substituted for another with which it is closely associated. Unlike metaphors, which involve a direct comparison, metonyms rely on the idea of proximity or association. The substituted term is typically something related to, but not the same as, the original term.

For example, using "the crown" to refer to a monarch or royalty, or "the White House" to refer to the U.S. government or presidency. Metonyms are often used for brevity, emphasis, or rhetorical effect. They can evoke specific associations or connotations, drawing attention to particular aspects or qualities of the thing being referenced. Metonyms are common in everyday language, literature, journalism, and political discourse, where they serve to convey complex ideas or situations succinctly and vividly.

"Mood- or Consciousness-altering Techniques and Substances" refer to practices or substances that can modify a person's mental state, emotions, or consciousness. These techniques and substances can have a wide range of effects, from mild alterations in mood to profound changes in perception and cognition.

Some common examples include:

- Psychoactive drugs like alcohol and cannabis.
- Psychedelics such as LSD and psilocybin.
- Practices like meditation and mindfulness.
- Breathwork techniques.
- Hypnosis.
- Music and sound therapy.
- Light therapy.

These methods can affect mood, perception, and consciousness, but caution is advised due to potential risks and adverse effects.

"Moral Sentiments" refer to the emotions, attitudes, and intuitions that shape individuals' moral judgments and behaviors. They encompass feelings such as empathy, compassion, guilt, shame, and moral outrage, which guide individuals in evaluating the rightness or wrongness of their actions and those of others. Moral sentiments play a crucial role in ethical decision-making, interpersonal relationships, and social interactions, influencing how individuals perceive moral dilemmas, resolve conflicts, and uphold moral norms and values. Philosophers like Adam Smith and David Hume have explored the role of moral sentiments in moral philosophy, highlighting their importance in understanding human morality and moral reasoning.

"Morphemes" are the smallest units of meaning in a language. They can be words themselves or parts of words, such as prefixes, suffixes, and roots. Morphemes carry semantic information and can change the meaning or grammatical function of a word. For example, in the word "unhappiness," "un-" is a morpheme that indicates negation, "-ness" is a morpheme that denotes a state or quality, and "happy" is a morpheme that conveys the root meaning. Understanding morphemes is essential in linguistics for analyzing word formation, morphology, and the structure of languages.

"Taxonomy" is the science of classifying organisms into hierarchical groups based on their characteristics and evolutionary relationships. It involves organizing species into categories like genus, family, and kingdom, using binomial nomenclature. Taxonomy helps understand biodiversity and evolutionary history, guiding research and conservation efforts.

"Mourning" is the process of grieving the loss of someone or something significant. It involves experiencing and expressing emotions such as sadness, sorrow, and anguish in response to the death or absence of a loved one, the end of a relationship, or other significant losses. Mourning can take various forms, including rituals, ceremonies, and personal expressions of remembrance and commemoration. It plays a crucial role in coping with loss, processing emotions, and adapting to life changes, ultimately facilitating healing and acceptance. Cultural and religious customs often influence mourning practices, providing rituals and traditions to support individuals and communities through the grieving process.

"Murder proscribed" likely refers to the prohibition or condemnation of murder. In legal and ethical contexts, murder is universally condemned as a serious crime involving the unlawful killing of another person with malicious intent. Laws and moral codes in most societies prohibit murder and prescribe severe penalties for those convicted of committing this act.

The proscription of murder serves to protect individuals' right to life, maintain social order, and uphold justice within a community. It reflects fundamental ethical principles regarding the value of human life, the importance of respecting others' rights, and the need to prevent harm and violence.

The prohibition against murder is enshrined in legal systems worldwide, with specific laws defining murder, establishing degrees of culpability, and outlining appropriate punishments. In addition to legal consequences, moral and social condemnation often accompany acts of murder, reflecting broader societal norms and values regarding the sanctity of life and the inherent worth of every individual.

"Myths" are traditional stories that explain natural phenomena or cultural practices. They involve gods, heroes, and symbols, passed down orally and often associated with religious beliefs. Myths convey cultural identity, morals, and narratives through symbolism and narrative structure. Examples are found in many cultures, shaping literature and art.

"Narrative" is the structured telling of a story, involving characters, plot, setting, and themes. It can take various forms like literature, film, or oral storytelling and serves purposes such as entertainment and conveying messages. Narratives help us make sense of the world and connect with others through storytelling.

"Nomenclature" is the system of naming things, especially in science. It ensures consistency and clarity in communication by assigning names or labels to objects, organisms, and concepts. In biology, binomial nomenclature, developed by Linnaeus, assigns two-part Latin names to species. Overall, nomenclature organizes knowledge and facilitates communication within scientific fields.

"Onomatopoeia" is a linguistic device where words imitate or evoke the sounds associated with the objects or actions they describe. In other words, the word itself sounds like the noise it represents. Examples of onomatopoeic words include "buzz," "meow," "boom," "hiss," and "sizzle." Onomatopoeia is commonly used in literature, poetry, and everyday language to create vivid imagery, enhance sensory experiences, and evoke emotions. It adds a layer of realism and immediacy to the written or spoken word, allowing readers or listeners to better visualize and engage with the text.

Taryn Elliott

"Non-bodily Decorative Art" encompasses creative expressions that adorn objects or spaces, excluding the human body. This category includes various forms such as:

Interior Design: Artistic arrangements of furniture, textiles, and decorative elements within interior spaces to enhance aesthetics and functionality.

Architecture: Designing and constructing buildings and structures with aesthetic appeal, incorporating decorative elements like facades, ornaments, and landscaping.

Visual Arts: Painting, sculpture, and other visual mediums used to create decorative pieces for display in homes, offices, and public spaces.

Decorative Crafts: Handmade objects such as ceramics, glassware, textiles, and jewelry designed for decorative purposes.

Decorative Arts: Art forms like pottery, metalwork, and woodworking that prioritize aesthetic appeal and craftsmanship.

Non-bodily decorative art plays a significant role in enhancing environments, reflecting cultural values, and providing aesthetic pleasure.

Pixabay

"Body Art" refers to artistic expressions that involve decorating or modifying the human body. It encompasses various forms, including:

- **Tattoos:** Permanent or temporary designs made by inserting ink or pigments into the skin using needles. Tattoos can range from small, simple designs to intricate, elaborate artworks covering large areas of the body.
- *Body Piercings:* Inserting jewelry or other decorative objects into piercings made in different parts of the body, such as the ears, nose, lips, tongue, eyebrows, and navel.
- *Body Painting:* Using paint, makeup, or other temporary materials to create designs or patterns directly on the skin. Body painting can be done for artistic, cultural, or ceremonial purposes.
- *Scarification:* Creating patterns or designs on the skin by intentionally scarring or cutting the skin in controlled ways. Scarification is practiced in some cultures for ritual, cultural, or decorative reasons.
- *Henna:* Applying natural dye made from the henna plant to create temporary designs on the skin, often used for celebratory or ceremonial occasions in various cultures.

Body art is a form of self-expression, cultural tradition, and personal adornment that has been practiced for centuries across different societies and civilizations. It can convey individual identity, social status, group affiliation, and cultural heritage, and serves as a means of communication and artistic creativity.

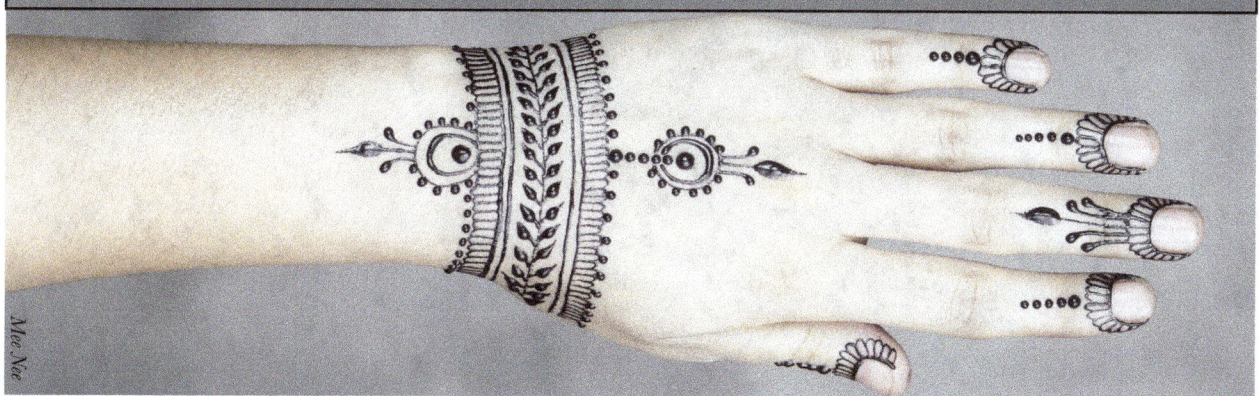

"Normal and Abnormal States" refer to variations in physical, mental, or behavioral conditions that deviate from what is considered typical or expected within a given context. These terms are often used in medical, psychological, and social contexts to describe the range of human experiences and functioning.

Normal States: Normal states refer to conditions or behaviors that are considered within the range of typical or healthy functioning for an individual or population.
These states may vary depending on factors such as age, culture, and environment. For example, feeling sad occasionally or experiencing mild anxiety before a stressful event may be considered normal emotional responses.

Abnormal States: Abnormal states, on the other hand, describe conditions or behaviors that fall outside the range of typical or healthy functioning and may indicate underlying physical, psychological, or social problems. These states may manifest as deviations from expected patterns of thoughts, emotions, behaviors, or physical symptoms. For example, persistent and severe feelings of sadness or anxiety that interfere with daily functioning may be considered abnormal and indicative of a mental health disorder.

It's important to note that the distinction between normal and abnormal states is not always clear-cut and may vary depending on individual differences, cultural norms, and societal expectations. Additionally, what is considered abnormal in one context may be considered normal in another.

Vlado Paunovic

"The Oedipus and the Electra Complex" are psychoanalytic concepts proposed by Sigmund Freud to describe the unconscious desires and conflicts that children experience during their psychosexual development.

Oedipus Complex: The Oedipus complex occurs during the phallic stage (ages 3 to 6) of psychosexual development in boys. It involves unconscious feelings of desire for the opposite-sex parent (typically the mother) and hostility or rivalry toward the same-sex parent (typically the father). Boys may experience jealousy toward their fathers and fear castration as punishment for their desires. Resolution of the Oedipus complex involves identification with the same-sex parent and the internalization of societal norms and values.

Electra Complex: The Electra complex is a parallel concept proposed by Carl Jung and later developed by Freud to describe a similar dynamic in girls. It involves unconscious feelings of desire for the opposite-sex parent (typically the father) and hostility or rivalry toward the same-sex parent (typically the mother). Girls may experience penis envy and resentment toward their mothers. Like boys, resolution of the Electra complex involves identification with the same-sex parent and the internalization of societal norms and values.

These concepts are controversial and have been critiqued for their gendered assumptions and lack of empirical evidence. However, they remain influential in psychoanalytic theory and continue to inform discussions about parent-child relationships, gender development, and unconscious motivations.

Bianca Van Dijk

"Oligarchy" is a form of governance in which power is concentrated in the hands of a small group of individuals or a select few families, often based on wealth, social status, or other privileged criteria. In oligarchic systems, the ruling elite hold disproportionate influence and control over political, economic, and social institutions, allowing them to maintain their dominance and perpetuate their interests.

Key characteristics of oligarchy include:

Limited Participation: Oligarchies restrict political participation and decision-making to a small subset of the population, excluding the majority from meaningful involvement in governance.

Wealth and Influence: Oligarchs typically possess significant wealth, resources, or social connections, which they leverage to maintain their power and influence over key institutions, such as government, business, and the media.

Inequality and Privilege: Oligarchic systems tend to exacerbate social and economic inequality, as power and resources are concentrated among the ruling elite, while the rest of the population may experience limited opportunities and access to basic necessities.

Authoritarian Tendencies: Oligarchies may exhibit authoritarian tendencies, as the ruling elite prioritize their own interests and seek to suppress dissent or opposition that threatens their control.

Oligarchies can take various forms, including aristocratic oligarchies (ruled by a hereditary aristocracy), plutocratic oligarchies (dominated by wealthy individuals or corporations), and military oligarchies (controlled by a small group of military leaders). While oligarchies may claim to represent the interests of the elite, they often face challenges from opposition movements advocating for greater democracy, accountability, and social justice.

"Overestimating the Objectivity of Thought" refers to the tendency for individuals to believe that their judgments, opinions, or interpretations of reality are more unbiased and rational than they actually are. This cognitive bias can lead people to trust their own perceptions and assessments without critically evaluating their underlying assumptions, biases, or limitations.

Key aspects of overestimating objectivity include:

Confirmation Bias: People may selectively perceive or interpret information in a way that confirms their preexisting beliefs or expectations, while dismissing or ignoring evidence that contradicts them.

Subjective Experience: Despite the subjective nature of human perception and cognition, individuals may mistakenly believe that their thoughts and judgments are objective reflections of reality, rather than influenced by personal biases, emotions, or experiences.

Cognitive Dissonance: When faced with information or viewpoints that challenge their existing beliefs, individuals may experience cognitive dissonance, a psychological discomfort that leads them to resist changing their opinions or considering alternative perspectives.

Illusion of Control: People may overestimate their ability to control or predict events, attributing outcomes to their own actions or decisions rather than recognizing the role of chance or external factors.

Belief in Rationality: Some individuals may have a strong faith in the power of reason and logic to guide their thinking, leading them to overlook the emotional, intuitive, or unconscious influences that shape their perceptions and judgments.

Overestimating objectivity can have significant implications in various domains, including decision-making, problem-solving, and interpersonal relationships. Recognizing and mitigating this bias requires self-awareness, critical thinking skills, and openness to considering alternative viewpoints and interpretations.

"Past, Present, and Future" are the three temporal dimensions that organize our experience of time.

Past: The past refers to events, experiences, and phenomena that have already occurred. It encompasses everything that has happened before the present moment, including personal memories, historical events, and the evolution of societies and civilizations.
The past shapes our identities, influences our perceptions and attitudes, and provides context for understanding the present and anticipating the future.

Present: The present is the current moment in time, the "now" in which we exist and experience the world. It is constantly shifting and evolving as time progresses, encompassing our immediate sensory experiences, thoughts, feelings, and actions. The present is where we engage with reality, make decisions, and interact with others.

Future: The future refers to events, possibilities, and outcomes that have not yet occurred but are anticipated to happen at some point beyond the present moment. It encompasses our hopes, goals, plans, and expectations for what lies ahead. The future is inherently uncertain and subject to change, influenced by various factors such as our actions, decisions, and external circumstances.

These temporal dimensions are interconnected and shape our understanding of time and our place within it. While the past informs our understanding of where we come from, the present is where we live and act, and the future represents our aspirations and potential directions. Balancing our engagement with the past, present, and future is essential for leading meaningful and purposeful lives.

"Planning" is the process of setting goals, determining actions, and allocating resources to achieve desired outcomes in the future. It involves anticipating future needs, challenges, and opportunities, and developing strategies to address them effectively. Key aspects of planning include:

Goal Setting: Identifying specific, measurable, achievable, relevant, and time-bound (SMART) objectives that align with organizational or personal priorities.

Analysis and Assessment: Conducting thorough research and evaluation to understand current conditions, identify strengths and weaknesses, and assess potential risks and opportunities.

Strategy Development: Formulating plans and tactics to achieve goals, considering factors such as timelines, resource availability, constraints, and potential obstacles.

Resource Allocation: Allocating human, financial, and material resources efficiently and effectively to support planned activities and initiatives.

Implementation and Monitoring: Executing planned activities and continuously monitoring progress, making adjustments as needed to stay on track and address emerging issues.

Evaluation and Feedback: Assessing the effectiveness of plans and strategies, gathering feedback from stakeholders, and using insights to inform future planning efforts.

Effective planning is essential for organizations and individuals to navigate uncertainty, manage change, and achieve success in their endeavors. It provides a roadmap for action, enhances decision-making, and promotes accountability and alignment across stakeholders. By investing time and effort in thoughtful planning, individuals and organizations can increase their likelihood of achieving their goals and realizing their visions for the future.

"Poetry and Rhetoric" are both forms of language artistry that aim to convey ideas, emotions, or aesthetics through words. While they share some similarities, they also have distinct characteristics and purposes:

Poetry: Poetry is a literary genre characterized by heightened language, rhythmic patterns, and imaginative expression. It often employs various literary devices such as metaphor, simile, imagery, and symbolism to evoke emotions, create vivid imagery, and convey complex meanings in a condensed form. Poetry can take many forms, including sonnets, haiku, free verse, and narrative poetry, each with its own structure and conventions. It is valued for its aesthetic qualities, emotional resonance, and ability to evoke profound insights into the human experience.

Rhetoric: Rhetoric is the art of persuasion and effective communication. It involves using language strategically to influence, persuade, or convince an audience of a particular point of view or argument. Rhetorical techniques include using logical reasoning, emotional appeals, and persuasive language to engage and persuade listeners or readers. Rhetoric is often employed in speeches, debates, essays, and other forms of public discourse to sway opinions, shape perceptions, and mobilize action. While rhetoric is primarily concerned with persuading and convincing, it can also be used to entertain, inform, or inspire.

In summary, poetry and rhetoric are both powerful forms of language artistry that engage with words and language to evoke emotions, convey ideas, and influence audiences. While poetry emphasizes creativity, imagery, and aesthetic expression, rhetoric focuses on persuasion, argumentation, and effective communication. Despite their differences, both poetry and rhetoric are integral to human communication and expression, enriching our understanding of language and its impact on society.

"Play to Perfect Skill" emphasizes the importance of incorporating playfulness and enjoyment into the process of skill development and mastery.

Here's how you can approach it:

Embrace Playfulness: Approach practice with a playful mindset, allowing yourself to explore, experiment, and make mistakes without fear of judgment.

Enjoy the Process: Focus on enjoying the process of learning and improvement, rather than solely fixating on achieving a specific outcome or level of proficiency.

Be Curious and Creative: Explore different approaches, techniques, and variations of the skill, and allow yourself to be curious and creative in your exploration.

Set Challenges and Goals: Set yourself challenges and goals that are motivating and engaging, providing a sense of accomplishment and progress as you work towards them.

Maintain Balance: While playfulness is important, balance it with focused and deliberate practice to ensure steady progress and improvement in your skill development journey.

Celebrate Successes: Celebrate your successes and achievements along the way, no matter how small, and use them as fuel to keep you motivated and inspired to continue playing and perfecting your skills.

By infusing playfulness into your practice sessions, you can foster a positive and enjoyable learning experience that enhances your motivation, creativity, and overall skill development.

"Pride" is a complex emotion that involves a sense of satisfaction, self-respect, and fulfillment in one's own achievements, qualities, or identity. It can manifest in various forms, including pride in oneself, one's accomplishments, one's community or culture, or one's values and beliefs. While pride can be a positive and empowering emotion, it can also become problematic when it becomes excessive or narcissistic. Here are some key aspects of pride:

Positive Pride: Positive pride arises from genuine accomplishments, efforts, or characteristics that one values and takes satisfaction in. It can boost self-esteem, confidence, and motivation, encouraging individuals to strive for excellence and pursue their goals with determination.

Collective Pride: Collective pride involves a sense of attachment and identification with a group, community, or culture, leading individuals to feel a sense of solidarity and belonging based on shared values, traditions, or achievements.

Healthy Pride: Healthy pride involves a balanced and realistic appreciation of one's strengths, accomplishments, and identity. It acknowledges individual worth and dignity without diminishing or denigrating others.

Excessive Pride: Excessive pride, also known as hubris or arrogance, involves an inflated sense of superiority, entitlement, or self-importance. It can lead to feelings of superiority over others, intolerance of differing viewpoints, and a lack of empathy or humility.

Vulnerable Pride: Vulnerable pride arises from a fragile sense of self-esteem or identity, leading individuals to seek validation and approval from others to bolster their self-worth. It can result in feelings of insecurity, defensiveness, or resentment in response to perceived threats or criticism.

Ultimately, pride is a natural and universal human emotion that plays a significant role in shaping individual and collective identities, values, and behaviors. When experienced in moderation and in conjunction with humility and empathy, pride can be a positive force for personal growth, social cohesion, and cultural enrichment.

A **"Private Inner Life"** refers to the thoughts, feelings, beliefs, desires, and experiences that an individual keeps to themselves and does not readily share with others. It encompasses the inner world of thoughts, emotions, and reflections that occur within a person's mind and consciousness, often away from public scrutiny or observation.

Key aspects of a private inner life include:

- *Personal Reflection:* Engaging in introspection and self-reflection to explore one's thoughts, emotions, and experiences, gaining insight into one's identity, values, and motivations.
- *Emotional Depth:* Experiencing a range of emotions, both positive and negative, and processing them internally before choosing to express or share them with others.
- *Inner Dialogue:* Engaging in internal dialogue or self-talk to process information, make decisions, and navigate life's challenges, conflicts, and uncertainties.
- *Creative Expression:* Tapping into one's imagination, creativity, and intuition to generate ideas, insights, and inspirations that contribute to personal growth, self-expression, and artistic endeavors.
- *Spiritual Exploration:* Exploring questions of meaning, purpose, and existence through spiritual or philosophical inquiry, seeking deeper understanding and connection with oneself and the world.
- *Boundary Setting:* Establishing boundaries and limits around one's private inner life, determining what thoughts, emotions, and experiences are shared with others and what remains personal and confidential.
- *Self-Care:* Practicing self-care and self-nurturing activities that promote well-being, balance, and harmony within one's inner world, such as meditation, mindfulness, journaling, or engaging in hobbies and interests.

A rich and vibrant private inner life is essential for personal growth, self-awareness, and psychological well-being. It provides individuals with a sanctuary for self-discovery, self-expression, and self-fulfillment, fostering a deeper sense of authenticity, autonomy, and resilience in navigating life's joys and challenges.

Karolina Grabowska

"Proverbs and Sayings"

are short, traditional expressions of wisdom, advice, or cultural beliefs that convey moral lessons, practical knowledge, or social norms. They often reflect the values, beliefs, and experiences of a particular culture or community and are passed down orally from generation to generation. Here are a few examples:

- *A stitch in time saves nine*: It's better to deal with a problem early on before it becomes more serious and difficult to solve.
- *Actions speak louder than words*: What people do is more important than what they say.
- *All good things must come to an end:* Nothing lasts forever; eventually, everything will come to an end or change.
- *Birds of a feather flock together:* People tend to associate with others who are similar to themselves in character, interests, or background.
- *Don't count your chickens before they hatch*: Don't make plans or assumptions based on something that hasn't happened yet.
- *Every cloud has a silver lining:* Even in difficult or challenging situations, there is always something positive or hopeful to be found.
- *Honesty is the best policy:* It's better to be truthful and straightforward in all situations.
- *Look before you leap:* Think carefully and consider the consequences before taking action.
- *The early bird catches the worm:* Being proactive and taking action early can lead to success or opportunities.
- *Where there's a will, there's a way:* If someone is determined and motivated enough, they can find a solution to any problem.

These proverbs and sayings often serve as moral guidelines, practical advice, or cautionary tales, offering timeless wisdom that is applicable across different cultures and contexts.

"Psychological Defense Mechanisms" are unconscious strategies or patterns of thought that individuals use to cope with anxiety, stress, or threats to their self-esteem. These mechanisms operate outside of conscious awareness and help individuals manage uncomfortable or distressing emotions by distorting reality, minimizing psychological discomfort, or regulating internal conflicts. Here are some common defense mechanisms:

- *Denial:* Refusing to acknowledge or accept the reality of a situation or experience.
- *Projection:* Attributing one's own unacceptable thoughts, feelings, or motives to others.
- *Rationalization:* Creating logical explanations or justifications to make unacceptable behaviors or situations seem more acceptable.
- *Regression:* Reverting to earlier, more immature behaviors or coping mechanisms in response to stress or anxiety.
- *Displacement:* Redirecting emotions, thoughts, or impulses from their original target to a less threatening or more acceptable substitute target.
- *Sublimation:* Channeling unacceptable impulses or emotions into socially acceptable activities or behaviors.
- *Reaction Formation:* Expressing feelings or beliefs that are the opposite of one's true feelings or beliefs, often to conceal or manage unacceptable impulses.
- *Intellectualization:* Avoiding uncomfortable emotions by focusing excessively on intellectual or abstract thoughts or concepts.
- *Suppression:* Consciously avoiding or pushing aside thoughts, feelings, or memories that are too distressing to confront.
- *Undoing:* Engaging in behaviors or rituals to try to "undo" or reverse the perceived negative consequences of one's actions or thoughts.

These defense mechanisms serve as automatic psychological strategies to protect the individual from psychological discomfort, maintain self-esteem, and regulate internal conflicts. While they can be helpful in managing short-term stress or anxiety, overreliance on defense mechanisms can interfere with emotional growth, interpersonal relationships, and overall psychological well-being.

"Territoriality" refers to the innate tendency of individuals or groups to establish and defend territory as their own. Here's a concise overview:

Definition: Territoriality involves the behavior of marking, defending, and controlling a physical space, area, or boundary, whether it's a home, workplace, or social environment.

Purpose: It serves various purposes, including providing security, resources, and a sense of identity, belonging, and control over one's environment.

Manifestations: Territorial behavior can manifest in different ways, such as marking boundaries, displaying aggression towards intruders, or using territorial signals like scent marking or vocalization.

Social Constructs: Territoriality is not limited to animals; humans also exhibit territorial behavior, often expressing ownership and attachment to spaces through property rights, boundaries, and personalization.

Implications: Territorial behavior can have social, psychological, and ecological implications, influencing social interactions, resource distribution, and environmental management.

Overall, territoriality is a fundamental aspect of behavior in both humans and animals, playing a significant role in shaping social dynamics, resource allocation, and the organization of space.

"Trade" is the exchange of goods and services between individuals, businesses, or nations. It allows for the efficient allocation of resources, fosters economic growth, and promotes cooperation globally. Through trade, parties benefit from specialization and access to a wider range of goods and services. Governments regulate trade through policies such as tariffs and subsidies, and trade plays a key role in globalization by connecting economies and cultures worldwide.

"Tools" are implements or instruments used to perform specific tasks or achieve certain objectives. They can be physical objects, such as hammers, screwdrivers, or wrenches, designed for manual use, or they can be digital devices, software programs, or methodologies used in various fields or industries. Tools enhance human capabilities, streamline processes, and increase efficiency and productivity. They can range from simple handheld tools to complex machinery or sophisticated software applications. Whether used in construction, manufacturing, agriculture, healthcare, or technology, tools play a vital role in enabling individuals and organizations to accomplish tasks more effectively and achieve their goals.

"Time" is the measure of the duration and sequence of events. It flows continuously from past to present to future. People perceive and experience time subjectively, influenced by culture, context, and individual factors. Effective time management is crucial for productivity and achieving goals. Time is also a subject of study in physics and philosophy, with concepts like relativity and causality.

Paula Schmidt

"Rituals" are symbolic actions, behaviors, or ceremonies that hold cultural, religious, or social significance and are performed in a prescribed manner. They often involve repetitive gestures, words, or practices and serve various purposes within societies or groups. Here's a brief overview:

- *Cultural and Religious Significance:* Rituals play a central role in cultural and religious traditions, serving to mark important milestones, express beliefs and values, and strengthen social bonds within communities.
- *Symbolism and Meaning:* Rituals often involve symbolic elements that represent deeper meanings or convey specific messages. These symbols may relate to spirituality, identity, mythology, or shared cultural heritage.
- *Social Cohesion:* Rituals help foster a sense of belonging and solidarity among
- participants by reinforcing shared beliefs, values, and norms. They contribute to social cohesion and group identity by creating a sense of continuity and tradition.
- *Life Transitions:* Many rituals are associated with life transitions, such as birth, puberty, marriage, and death. These rites of passage help individuals navigate significant life
- changes and provide a framework for understanding and coping with transitions.
- *Healing and Transformation:* Rituals can serve as mechanisms for healing,
- transformation, or catharsis by providing individuals with a structured way to process
- emotions, experiences, or trauma.
- *Community and Connection:* Participating in rituals fosters a sense of connection and communion with others, whether through shared prayers, ceremonies, or rituals of solidarity and support.

Overall, rituals are an integral part of human culture and social life, providing individuals and communities with a sense of meaning, identity, and belonging. They help reinforce social norms, transmit cultural values, and provide a framework for understanding and navigating the complexities of life.

Todd Trapani

"Negative Reciprocity", also known as revenge or retaliation, refers to the act of responding to perceived harm or injustice with a similar or greater degree of harm or wrongdoing.

Here's a brief explanation:

Definition: Negative reciprocity involves seeking retribution or vengeance in response to a perceived offense, injury, or injustice inflicted by another individual or group.

Motivation: Negative reciprocity is often driven by feelings of anger, resentment, or a desire for justice or revenge. Individuals may seek retaliation as a way to restore their sense of power, dignity, or fairness.

Forms: Negative reciprocity can take various forms, including verbal attacks, physical violence, sabotage, or seeking legal or social consequences for the perceived wrongdoer.

Consequences: While negative reciprocity may provide temporary satisfaction or relief, it often perpetuates cycles of conflict, harm, and escalation. It can lead to further retaliation, escalation of tensions, and deterioration of relationships or social cohesion.

Alternatives: In many cases, seeking positive forms of reciprocity, such as forgiveness, conflict resolution, or reconciliation, can lead to more constructive outcomes and help break cycles of retaliation and conflict.

In summary, negative reciprocity involves responding to perceived harm or injustice with retaliatory actions or behaviors, driven by feelings of anger, resentment, or a desire for retribution. While it may offer temporary satisfaction, it often leads to further harm and conflict, highlighting the importance of seeking constructive alternatives to resolve disputes and promote reconciliation.

"Shame" is a powerful and often painful emotion characterized by feelings of embarrassment, guilt, or humiliation resulting from a perceived failure, mistake, or social transgression. It involves a negative evaluation of oneself and can be triggered by internal factors such as personal beliefs or external factors such as societal norms or judgment from others. Shame often leads to a desire to hide or withdraw from social interactions and can have significant psychological and emotional effects on individuals, impacting self-esteem, relationships, and overall well-being. However, it can also serve as a signal to recognize and address areas for personal growth or change.

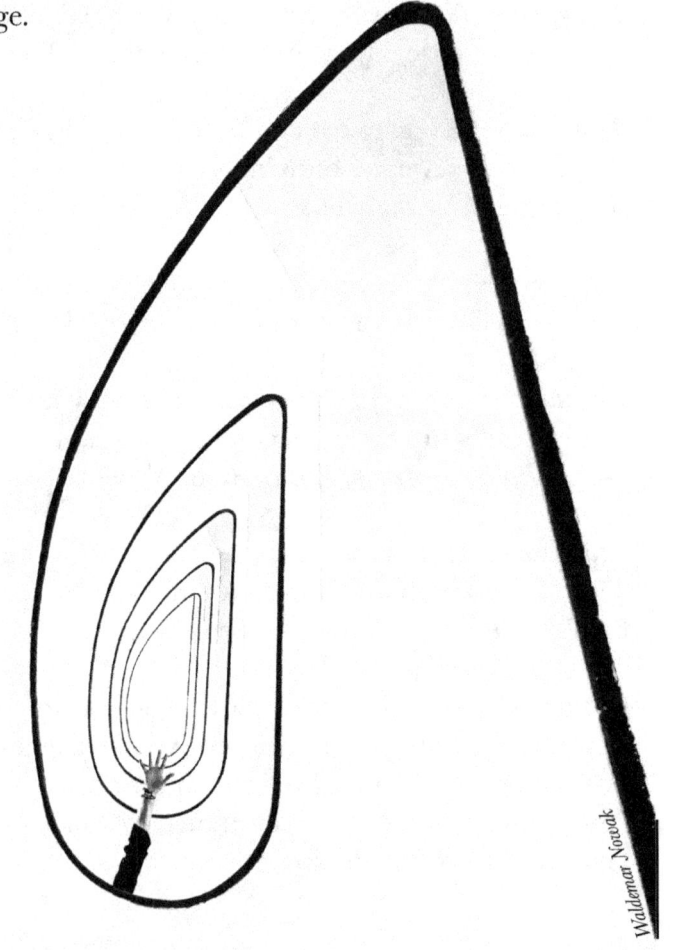

"Risk-taking" involves engaging in uncertain actions or decisions with potential positive or negative outcomes. Motivated by excitement or reward, individuals pursue opportunities despite potential harm. It varies among people and contexts, with benefits including personal growth and innovation, balanced against the risk of failure or harm.

"Shelter" refers to a place or structure that provides protection and safety from environmental elements, such as weather, and potential threats, such as animals or other dangers. It serves as a basic human need, offering refuge and security for individuals and families. Shelters can vary widely in form, from simple structures like tents or makeshift dwellings to more permanent buildings like houses or apartments. The provision of shelter is essential for ensuring the well-being and survival of individuals, particularly in times of crisis or adversity.

"Violence" refers to the use of physical force, intimidation, or coercion to cause harm, injury, or damage to individuals, groups, or property. It can take various forms, including physical violence (such as assault, battery, or homicide), verbal violence (such as threats, insults, or harassment), and symbolic violence (such as discrimination, oppression, or systemic injustice). Violence can occur in interpersonal relationships, communities, or on a larger societal scale, and it often stems from underlying factors such as conflict, power imbalances, social inequalities, or unresolved grievances. Addressing and preventing violence requires efforts to promote nonviolent conflict resolution, foster empathy and understanding, address root causes of violence, and create safe and supportive environments for all individuals and communities.

"Succession" refers to the process of one entity replacing another in a specific role, position, or status. Here's a concise overview:

Definition: Succession involves the orderly transition of power, authority, or ownership from one individual, group, or generation to another within an organization, institution, or family.

Types: There are various types of succession, including leadership succession (such as the transfer of leadership in a company or government), ecological succession (the gradual change of plant and animal communities in an ecosystem), and inheritance succession (the passing of property or assets from one generation to the next).

Process: Succession often involves formal procedures or protocols to ensure a smooth transition, such as appointing successors, establishing succession plans, or following legal protocols for inheritance.

Importance: Successful succession is crucial for maintaining continuity, stability, and effectiveness within organizations, ecosystems, and families. It ensures the preservation of values, knowledge, and resources over time.

Challenges: Succession can be challenging, particularly when there is uncertainty, conflict, or lack of preparation. Effective succession planning and communication are essential for mitigating risks and ensuring a successful transition.

In summary, succession is the process of replacing one entity with another in a particular role or position, essential for maintaining continuity and stability in various aspects of life.

"Socialization" is the process through which individuals learn and internalize the norms, values, beliefs, and behaviors of their culture or society. Here's a brief overview:

Definition: Socialization is the lifelong process of acquiring the skills, knowledge, and social behaviors necessary for participating effectively in society.

Agents: Socialization occurs through various agents, including family, peers, education, media, religion, and institutions. Each of these agents plays a role in shaping an individual's identity, attitudes, and understanding of the world.

Stages: Socialization occurs in stages throughout the lifespan, beginning in early childhood and continuing into adulthood. Different stages involve different socialization agents and focus on acquiring specific social roles and responsibilities.

Functions: Socialization serves several functions, including teaching individuals how to interact with others, navigate social norms and expectations, develop a sense of self and identity, and internalize cultural values and beliefs.

Cultural Variation: Socialization practices vary across cultures and societies, reflecting differences in values, beliefs, and social structures. Cultural norms and expectations shape the socialization process and influence individual development.

Impact: Socialization has a profound impact on individual behavior, attitudes, and relationships, influencing everything from language acquisition and gender roles to political beliefs and moral values.

> Overall, socialization is a fundamental aspect of human development, shaping the way individuals perceive themselves and others and guiding their interactions within society.

"Intellectual intelligence", often simply referred to as "intelligence," is the capacity for learning, understanding, reasoning, and problem-solving. Intellectual intelligence encompasses cognitive abilities related to learning, reasoning, and problem-solving, which are essential for navigating the complexities of the world and achieving personal and professional goals. Here's a concise explanation:

Learning and Understanding: Intellectual intelligence involves the ability to acquire knowledge, comprehend concepts, and grasp complex ideas across various domains, such as mathematics, language, science, and the humanities.

Reasoning: It encompasses logical thinking, critical analysis, and the ability to draw conclusions based on evidence, patterns, and principles. Intellectual intelligence enables individuals to make sound judgments and decisions.

Problem-Solving: Intellectual intelligence includes the skill to identify problems, evaluate different solutions, and apply effective strategies to overcome challenges or achieve goals. It involves creativity, adaptability, and innovation in finding solutions to novel or unfamiliar problems.

Measurement: Intellectual intelligence is often assessed through standardized tests, such as IQ tests, which measure cognitive abilities such as logical reasoning, verbal comprehension, and spatial awareness. However, it's important to note that intelligence is multifaceted and cannot be fully captured by a single test.

Application: Intellectual intelligence is crucial for success in education, work, and various aspects of daily life. It enables individuals to learn new skills, excel academically, perform effectively in professional settings, and adapt to changing circumstances.

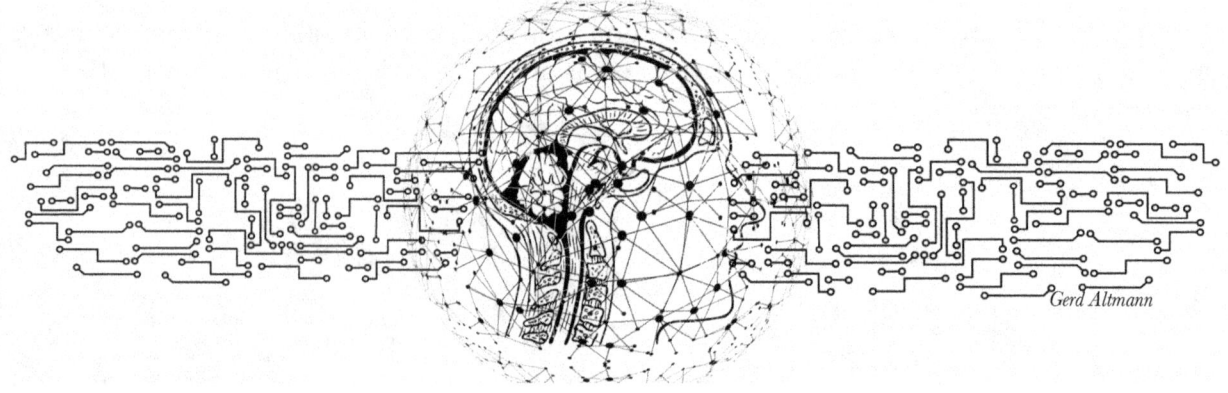

Gerd Altmann

"Emotional intelligence" refers to the ability to perceive, understand, manage, and express emotions effectively in oneself and others. Here's a brief overview:

Perception: EI involves recognizing and accurately identifying emotions in oneself and others, as well as understanding how emotions influence thoughts, behaviors, and relationships.
Understanding: It entails comprehending the causes and consequences of emotions, including the ability to empathize with others' perspectives and experiences.
Management: EI involves effectively regulating and controlling one's own emotions, as well as responding to the emotions of others in constructive and adaptive ways. This includes managing stress, handling interpersonal conflicts, and maintaining emotional resilience.
Expression: It encompasses the ability to express emotions appropriately and assertively, as well as to communicate feelings in a way that fosters understanding, connection, and cooperation.
Importance: Emotional intelligence is essential for personal and professional success, influencing various aspects of life, such as social relationships, leadership effectiveness, decision-making, and mental well-being.

> Emotional intelligence encompasses a range of abilities related to understanding and managing emotions, which are crucial for navigating life's challenges, fostering healthy relationships, and achieving personal and professional goals.

S...

"Symbolism" is using symbols to convey deeper meanings beyond their literal representation. It's found in art, literature, religion, and everyday life, enriching communication by evoking emotions and conveying abstract concepts through objects, colors, gestures, and more.

"Symbolic Speech" is nonverbal expression conveying a message or idea, protected as free speech. It includes gestures, signs, and actions like flag burning or wearing armbands for protest. It's crucial for political dissent and freedom of expression in democratic societies.

"Social Structure" refers to the organized patterns of relationships, roles, institutions, and norms within a society. It guides social interactions, shapes individual behavior, and influences societal stability and change.

Waldemar Nowak

"Triangular Awareness", in the context of assessing relationships among the self and two other people, typically involves examining the dynamics, interactions, and connections within a three-person relationship or social system. Here's a brief overview:

Self: This refers to one's own thoughts, feelings, perceptions, and behaviors within the context of the relationship triangle. It involves self-awareness, self-reflection, and understanding one's own role, needs, and motivations in the interaction.

Others: This involves considering the perspectives, experiences, and behaviors of the two other individuals involved in the relationship. It requires empathy, perspective-taking, and understanding the unique characteristics, desires, and contributions of each person.

Interactions: This encompasses the ways in which the three individuals interact, communicate, and influence each other within the relationship triangle. It involves observing patterns of communication, power dynamics, conflict resolution styles, and emotional exchanges among all parties involved.

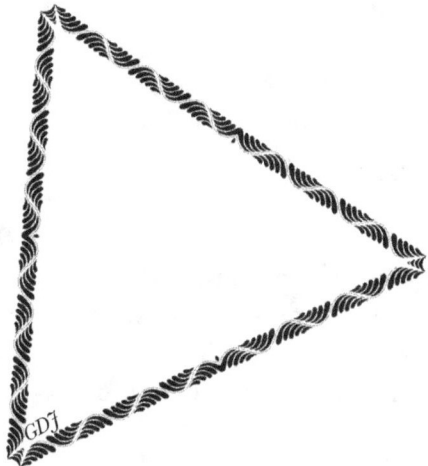

Assessing triangular awareness can provide insights into the complexities and nuances of interpersonal relationships, including the dynamics of love triangles, family systems, work teams, or social networks. By understanding the interactions and connections between oneself and two other individuals, individuals can gain deeper insight into their own relational patterns, improve communication and conflict resolution skills, and cultivate healthier and more fulfilling relationships.

Distinguishing between true and false involves the process of determining the accuracy or validity of statements, beliefs, or claims. Here's a brief overview:

True: A statement or belief is considered true if it corresponds with reality or accurately describes a situation, event, or fact as it actually exists. Truth is typically supported by evidence, logic, observation, or consensus within a relevant community or field.

False: A statement or belief is considered false if it does not correspond with reality or inaccurately describes a situation, event, or fact. Falsehoods may result from errors in perception, interpretation, or judgment, or they may be intentionally misleading or deceptive.

Distinguishing between true and false often requires critical thinking, skepticism, and the evaluation of evidence and sources. It involves considering multiple perspectives, seeking reliable information, and assessing the credibility and reliability of sources. Additionally, being open to revising one's beliefs in light of new evidence or information is essential for discerning truth from falsehood.

"Worldview", refers to the comprehensive framework of beliefs, values, assumptions, and perspectives through which individuals or groups interpret and make sense of the world around them. It shapes how people perceive reality, understand their place in the world, and navigate their lives. Key aspects of a worldview include:

- *Beliefs about Existence:* Views on the nature of reality, the origins of the universe, the existence of a higher power or spiritual dimension, and the purpose of human life.
- *Values and Ethics:* Principles and moral standards that guide behavior, decision-making, and interpersonal relationships, such as ideas about right and wrong, justice, freedom,
- and compassion.
- *Epistemology:* Perspectives on knowledge, truth, and the nature of understanding, including beliefs about the sources of knowledge (e.g., reason, faith, experience) and the reliability of different forms of knowledge (e.g., science, tradition, intuition).
- *Cosmology:* Views on the structure and organization of the universe, including beliefs about the natural world, the relationship between humanity and nature, and the
- interconnectedness of all things.
- *Human Nature:* Assumptions about the inherent characteristics, capacities, and
- potentialities of human beings, as well as beliefs about the nature of consciousness,
- identity, and personal agency.
- *Social and Cultural Constructs:* Perspectives on social institutions, cultural practices, norms, and identities, including beliefs about gender, ethnicity, class, and nationality.
- *Ontology:* Ideas about the nature of being and existence, including views on the
- distinction between mind and body, the existence of free will, and the nature of reality beyond empirical observation.

Worldviews are deeply ingrained and influence every aspect of human thought, behavior, and experience. They provide a framework for interpreting the world, making decisions, and finding meaning and purpose in life. While worldviews can vary widely across individuals, cultures, and historical periods, they play a fundamental role in shaping human identity, values, and worldview through which they interpret and engage with the world around them.

www.ingramcontent.com/pod-product-compliance
Lightning Source LLC
Chambersburg PA
CBHW080027130526
44591CB00037B/2698